D0205974

Laughing
at the
CIO

Advance Praise for *Laughing at the CIO ...*

"[This] book gives the CIO and everyone working professionally with information a recipe for identifying the critical success factors for unleashing the hidden values within your systems, and turning lifeless data into living and actionable information."
—Henrik Jeberg, CIO, Danish Ministry of Finance

"It is appalling that even today information is not treated as the valuable corporate asset it is. Except for a small number of obviously critical documents, most information assets are managed tactically rather than strategically, and almost always insufficiently. The only way to fix this is for senior executives to lead the charge—and this does not mean the Chief Information Officers all by themselves. Bob's respect within the information management consulting community combine with his communication and educational skills to make his newest book a must-read for any executive who cares about their company's value."
—Frank Gilbane, CEO, Gilbane Group Inc.

"Takes the mystery out of information management by providing practical, grounded solutions that reflect how people work with information, technology, and each other. ... Should be required reading for anyone already in or aspiring to be in a leadership position in an information-intensive organization."
—Mike Crandall, Chair and Senior Lecturer
Master of Science in Information Management Program
The Information School, University of Washington

"To move into the information age, we need to get the CIOs to become ambassadors of information, rather than technology. *Laughing at the CIO* illustrates very well the problem facing many organizations around the world, where the value and strategic impact of information is misunderstood or simply bluntly ignored. ... No matter what your title is, the book is highly recommended reading for all of those interested in the future well-being of their organizations."
—Janus Boye, Managing Director, Boye IT, and
principal author, Enterprise Portals Report

"Bob Boiko shows how and why to put the I back in IT. It's about time this book got written."
—Louis Rosenfeld, co-author, *Information Architecture for the World Wide Web*

"*Laughing at the CIO* is a very helpful book. I've been using Bob Boiko's tips and ideas in my day-to-day work with great success."
—Agueda Sánchez, MSIM 2005 Alumna
The Information School, University of Washington

LAUGHING at the CIO

A PARABLE AND PRESCRIPTION FOR IT LEADERSHIP

Bob Boiko

CyberAge Books

Information Today, Inc.
Medford, New Jersey

First printing, 2007

Laughing at the CIO: A Parable and Prescription for IT Leadership

Library of Congress Cataloging-in-Publication Data

Boiko, Bob.
　Laughing at the CIO : a parable and prescription for IT leadership / Bob Boiko.
　　p. cm.
　Includes index.
　ISBN 978-0-910965-78-1
　1.　Chief information officers. 2.　Information technology--Management 3.　Leadership. I. Title.

　HD30.2.B637 2007
　658.4'038--dc22

2007012461

Printed and bound in the United States of America.

President and CEO: Thomas H. Hogan, Sr.
Editor-in-Chief and Publisher: John B. Bryans
Managing Editor: Amy M. Reeve
VP Graphics and Production: M. Heide Dengler
Book Designer: Kara Mia Jalkowski
Cover Design: Lisa Boccadutre
Copy Editor: Barbara Brynko
Proofreader: Pat Hadley-Miller
Indexer: Sharon Hughes

This book is dedicated to the many managers who laughed,
moaned, or told me I was crazy when I suggested that
they get their executives to think strategically about information.

Contents

Figures and Tables

Figures

Tables

Acknowledgments

This book contains my first published work of fiction. The ballad of Les Knowles was harder to write than 10 times as much technology concept and methodology. If it was not for the expert eye and practiced patience of my editor John Burdick, I'd still be working on it and it would still not be a real story. John, also an accomplished technical writer, provided invaluable review and revision of the rest of the work. Karl Weyrauch also provided excellent feedback and revisions on the earliest drafts of the parable. Thanks, Karl and John.

In addition to John's professional review, I had comments and suggestions from a wide range of people in the field. In particular, I'd like to thank Claire Boiko, Tim Brennan, Agueda Sanchez, Jane McConnell, Liz Orna, Joseph Anderson, Mark C. Thompson, Rita Warren, Janus Boye, Martin White, Erik M. Hartman, Peter Morville, Jim Larkin, James Robertson, Brendan Quinn, and Tony Byrne. In addition, I'd like to thank the staff at the Library of Congress for their help finding and using the cartoons in this book.

The staff at Information Today, Inc. was good to me and great to work with. In particular, I'd like to thank John Bryans for his good nature, ready ear, and forward thinking. Amy Reeve was as nice as she was thorough as she shepherded the work through a long and tortuous process.

Of course, if it were not for the support and encouragement of my wife Laura McCormick and my sons Corey and Scotty, I would never have even begun this project.

Introduction: Learn to Care About Information

This book offers a set of ideas and methods that you can use to lead information creation, management, and distribution in your organization. More importantly, it helps you figure out how to turn information into the asset it is supposed to be.

Information management is often practiced as a combination of mumbo jumbo and voodoo. You can do much better!

This is a book for people who want to care about information but who don't entirely know how. I wrote this book because I have met too many executives and other "information leaders" who say they care about information but aren't doing anything about it. Obviously, someone named the Chief Information Officer (CIO) ought to care about information, but even among the chiefs, precious few actually take charge of information. Despite their titles, they avoid information like the plague. Some redefine "information" as just more data. Some consider information to be no more than a sideshow to the technology initiatives they really care about. Others hire staff with appropriate sounding titles such as "information architect" and "content manager" and then leave them to figure out what information is and what to do with it. This book helps information leaders lead. To appreciate what I have to say, however, you don't need to be a chief or even an executive; you just need to believe that information is power, and you have to want to harness some of that power for your organization.

I have never met an executive who disagrees with the idea that information is critical to the objectives of her organization. No executive that I know thinks that information is value-less or unworthy of investment. Everyone agrees that information is power. Everyone believes that we are in the Information Age. Everyone calls information a "strategic asset." So why have so few information leaders been able to harness the power of information? I suspect they don't know how.

This book shows you how. It presents you with a set of ideas and methods that you can use to lead information creation, management, and distribution in your organization. More importantly, it helps you figure out how to turn information into the asset it is supposed to be.

Our executives would not have become executives if they did not know about finance. They are personally responsible for budgeting and disbursing a lot of money. They would never ignore their responsibility for the strategic management of financial assets. Similarly, they would not have become executives without plenty of management experience. They cannot ignore their responsibility to define their staff and align them with their organization's goals. If information is the "organizational lifeblood" that everyone makes it out to be, then why shouldn't our executives be skilled at information as well? They should, of course, and they would if they only knew how.

All executives should understand how information works, but at least one should lead. An information leader tells her executive peers and managers what information has to do with the success of the organization. She has a well-formed information strategy that spells it out in terms that are easy to understand.

Within her own group (IT, IS, ICT, what have you), the information leader tells her managers and practitioners what sorts of systems to build to help the organization the most. Without this leadership, managers and practitioners build systems that may or may not actually help. Today, too many good managers and practitioners are left to develop their own information strategy and sell it to disinterested executives. Other less enlightened managers go forward with no strategy at all, and their projects meander like rudderless ships.

This book will help you get on top of information and ahead of information projects and technology. I present the concepts, models, and practices you need to inspire and lead information projects. I take a practical approach to crafting and carrying out information strategy, ensuring that you are never without a clear direction for your work or something constructive to say about information systems and how they help your organization.

It's actually not so hard to figure out what information can do for your organization. It is much harder to get information to do what you decided it should. Still, there are solid steps you can take to assure that the information systems you create result in benefits to your organization. In addition, there are fairly simple mental models you can use to understand and direct most of the common information endeavors in your organization including intranets, portals, knowledge management systems, and the many other management systems you have or need.

We are at the bare beginning of the Information Age, so be patient with your staff, your executive peers, and particularly with yourself. Everyone (myself included) is still figuring out what it means to manage information. All of our careers will be spent continually trying and failing to get information under control. But on the heels of each failure we will build more understanding and master more tools.

If you don't like being in that sort of situation, you might as well stop reading now and consider finding another profession. But if you do read on, I promise to give you a set of tools you can use to lead information management. Along the way, these same tools, and the perspective they provide, might put you in a position to lead more than just information.

Who Is This Book For?

This book is for anyone who wants to lead information management in her organization. Many organizations have a designated Chief Information Officer (CIO). In organizations that don't, the person in charge of information is called something else (vice president, executive vice president, or director, for example). Regardless of the title, the information leader is the one between policy and action, strategy and tactics, leadership and management. She is responsible for making sure that information is done well in her organization.

This book is for information leaders and leader wannabes. If you are in a leadership position, you can use the information I provide to stay there. If you are not in a leadership position, you can use this information to get there.

Executives

This book is written for you, but since I don't know you personally, I'll have to make some assumptions. First, I assume that information management has generally meant technology to you. You tend to interact relatively little with the information that gets managed and more with the system that does the managing. I'll try to convince you, however, that understanding the structure and delivery of information is just as important as understanding the systems. In fact, such an understanding is the main advantage you can have over your executive peers. It can even be the basis for your position of respect and leadership.

Second, I assume that you don't have the time or the inclination to read long academic works or learn elaborate methodologies. So, I'll try to boil down what you need to know and present it in short segments that can be consumed quickly and applied somewhat independently.

Finally, I assume that I can help you most by giving you information you can use immediately in the next meeting you have with your staff, peers, or bosses. So I will present mental models, practical processes, questions to ask, and answers to give.

You need to keep control of information initiatives without being dragged into running them directly. For this purpose, I'll try to give you an attitude, a philosophy, and a set of guiding principles to ensure that your projects are on track and will deliver solid value against the goals of your organization.

Managers

I suspect that you will be most interested in this book if you are leading an information initiative without executive support, if you want to "up-train" your executives, or if you aspire to be the executive in charge of information.

To lead without support or to become a leader, you can pretend to be the leader. Do what the leader does even if no one has given you any permission to do so. The one who successfully wears the mantle of information leadership eventually becomes the information leader (in duties at least, if not in rank).

You might also look at this book as a training manual for the people other than you who should be figuring out information strategy. It should not really be your job to figure all this out, but until you can get the right people to take the job off your hands, you will have to bring them along slowly, showing them what to do at each step. If your executives are already interested in information, you can learn to identify gaps in their approach. Then at the opportune moment, you will know exactly what to say to move her forward. You will also want to look closely at the advice I give executives for working with you. Are you ready to be asked the questions I propose that they ask you?

The best I can hope for is that this book passes frequently between you and your executives and helps you form a shared vision and plan of attack for managing information.

Other Readers

Even if you are not in a leadership position and even if you never aspire to be in one, this book can help you understand the wider context within which your projects operate. But be careful. If you know too much, you may end up as a leader anyway.

Project staff such as programmers, content creators and editors, administrators, information architects, publishers, and designers can all find insight into their own jobs in this book. Maybe you will see your projects in a new light. Maybe you can help others broaden their perspective beyond particular projects to the reason projects exist in the first place.

Students and academics studying information, computing, communication, or business might all be interested in reading on. I have taught a number of popular courses on the strategic use of information. It's a hot subject among technology as well as humanities students. As far as I'm concerned, students from just about any discipline could have a part in the creation of information systems. There are few practical texts on the subject; I am hoping that you will count this as one.

Business analysts and consultants who advise others on these matters should find plenty to think about here. Much of the interest I have seen in my work has been from people who help others figure out strategy. I have learned a lot from the methods and models you have worked out. Here, I present mine to you for your review and comment.

What's in This Book?

This book is an introduction to information management. It presents a way of thinking about information management and practical methodologies for making information management happen. The book follows this path:

- **Laughing at the CIO** – The first part of this book is half-parable and half-case study. Here, I describe and cut down a "straw man" organization in which information initiatives are created and fail at an alarming rate. The CIO is trapped between the unrealistic demands of his organization and his own lack of understanding of the demands of modern information systems. The story charts the decline of the CIO from a position of high hopes and respect into a mire or derision and ineffectuality. The story ends where the rest of the book begins: With the realization that modern information systems require a very different attitude and process, ones that the organization may or may not be ready for.

- **Get Perspective** – The second part of this book lays out a simple but powerful perspective on what information is and what it could mean to your organization.

- **Lead Up** – The third part of this book is about what you need to be an information executive: the concepts and the attitude. I lay out a straightforward approach to information governance and a simple technique you can use to create an enterprise strategy.

- **Lead Across** – The fourth part of the book discusses how you can get other parts of your organization to understand information and take responsibility for its creation and use.

- **Lead Down** – The final part of this book is about your group. It shows you how to translate enterprise information strategy into departmental strategy and tactics. It provides an overview to an approach to departmental leadership and describes project leadership techniques.

When you have finished reading this book, you ought to know enough to either begin a lifelong pursuit of orderly information or decide that managing information is the last thing you'd want to do. If you are already in the pursuit, I hope you come away with at least a few new ideas for your next move.

Who Am I?

I'm not an executive, although I have always thought like one. I am a consultant, teacher, businessman, programmer, and writer. (I am also a father, husband, friend, and colleague.)

Most of my clients are managers and practitioners. My authority and ability to speak to executives come from my frequent experience with ineffectual executive management and my less frequent experience with very effective executive management. I am often called upon to help a prospective client with technology. I inevitably end up helping them with information. The situation I hate the most is when my client can clearly see what needs to be done at the strategic level but has no access to the people at that level. I tell them to march into that office and tell that CIO what to do. But they just laugh. Some are so intimidated by their executives that they won't even let them know when they are about to fail.

I have taught undergraduate and graduate students the principles of information leadership, systems, and management. I have headed programs and defined curricula. I have admitted students in programs and later placed them in jobs. My favorite students are the ones who have been out in the world for a while, failing, and have come back to take a fresh look. My second favorite kind of student has no assumptions at all about what it means to design and build a system.

I've led various businesses for almost 20 years. I never set out to be a businessman. It happened to me when the company I was working for would not do what I told it to. I preferred leading no one to following anyone. From that point on, I've always had a business. I've grown them at dizzying rates and followed them down the tubes. I've held most of the jobs I talk about here but never in anyone else's organization. Today, I am once again in a business of one (well, two, if you count my wife) and happy to be there.

I've been programming since 1977 and worked as a programmer a number of times when I was younger. It was always a good way to bring in money when I was broke. The programming I like best is the sort where lots of nonprogrammers are involved—just the sort that you need to manage information.

Since finishing *Content Management Bible*, I have focused on helping organizations prepare for the long-term and massive task of repositioning their approach to information, publication, and communication. Along the way, I have formed some principles and practices that have helped those organizations make solid progress. This work is the result.

What Are Organizations?

When talking about information management, I always refer to organizations rather than to any particular form of organization (company, foundation, agency, and so on). While the information changes from organization to organization, information problems remain the same.

You can benefit from the advice I provide regardless of the kind of organization you are in or the purposes you are pursuing.

I've practiced information management in small nonprofits and Fortune 500 corporations, as well as in aerospace, health, retail, finance, manufacturing, software, and education. I've worked for governments and nongovernmental organizations (NGOs). I've worked in the Americas, Europe, Oceania, Africa, and Asia. I've always tried hard to understand my client's environment, but I've always been able to help them despite not being in their business. Across the world and in every organization, the same issues arise. How do we collect, manage, and distribute information in this wired world?

What Happened to Content Management?

I'm best known for the book *Content Management Bible* (Wiley, 2004), now in its second edition. When I wrote it, content management (CM) was just getting started. Today, it is well under way. Product offerings have matured (somewhat) and, more importantly, the people who need CM have begun to self-identify and are forming interest groups and communities. Many people now also have experience with a commercial CM product and are on their third or fourth go-round with building and rebuilding systems. If you have taken a broader and broader approach to what CM can do for an organization, this book is for you.

However, this is not a book about CM per se. While it has grown out of my concern with CM, the book takes a much wider perspective than one type of system can accommodate. In this book, I am pretty true to my previous work in content management. Many of the methods I propose here are natural extensions of those I have always advocated for in content management systems. So if your main concern is content, read on; it all applies. But beware: I will try to convince you to substitute the word "information" for "content" and to broaden your concern beyond just one sort of system.

On the other hand, I assume no prior familiarity with content or any other type of management. Instead, I build toward a general idea of information management that applies equally well to all the more specialized systems.

Why the Cartoons

I thought long and hard about how to illustrate this book. I wanted images that deepened the text and provided a strong counterpoint as well as an illustration of the concepts I was describing. I wanted images that were light and funny, but not silly. No Dilbert's for this text. I wanted images that had class, but were not stuffy. I wanted, everyone assured me, too much. Then I happened upon the American Cartoon Prints (cpam) and the French Political Cartoon collection at the U.S. Library of Congress (memory.loc.gov/pp). They were just right. They struck exactly the balance I was looking for. I knew

I was on the right track when I found myself paging through these cartoons just for the fun of it.

The cartoons I chose are from the U.S. and French political satirists of the 1800s. They depict the contradictions and contentions of their day. But flipping through these cartoons, it dawned on me that the contradictions and contentions of information strategy are the same. They are the issues that all would-be leaders face when they attempt to do something new or different. As you read on, look for Abraham Lincoln, Robert E. Lee, Benedict Arnold, U.S. Grant, and a host of other characters who could just as well be your co-workers as icons of U.S. history. If you are interested in learning more about these cartoons, go to www.laughingatthecio.com, where their sources and original captions are listed.

I'm also making a digital version of the book available at www.laughing atthecio.com. As a buyer of the print edition, this Laughing at the CIO ebook is available to you free of charge. (Please note, however, that the ebook is not a mirror image of the book, and that it is subject to change or discontinuation without notice.) Other ebooks—including those on information strategy and information department leadership that are referred to in this book—are also available on the site at a modest additional cost.

Part 1

Laughing at the CIO

I don't laugh at CIOs, but I know a lot of people who do. Mock-cronyms like "Career Is Over" and "Career in Obscurity" have hobbled the position and made it less attractive than it should be to both organizations and potential chiefs. Not long after CIOs finally took their place on the executive peak, the ground shifted and threw them off again. Some landed on their feet, some on their butts, but the position itself is still a little shaky. Their familiar territory of software, hardware, and local networks was blown wide open by global networks, unstructured data (what I call information), and the needy end users they themselves helped to create.

The position of CIO is a bit under the weather.
Information might just be the cure.

I'm old enough to have watched the whole thing unfold. When I started programming, we submitted decks of cards and time-shared on mainframes. IT (information technology) was brand new and unnamed. Systems operators (or SysOps) were mostly defectors from engineering and math. Few organizations outside of universities had computers at all, and if they did, only a select few professionals could get near them. The pocket-protector generation that grew IT from a cult to a major profession deserves credit. Thirty years later, due to the efforts of these early pioneers, computers are on every desktop and are all connected. Getting a computer on every desk, however, has changed the very fabric of their profession.

For a long time, being good at IT mostly meant tweaking hardware and running wires on the one hand, while designing, building, and loading software on the other. The life of an IT manager was not easy. Computer systems have always been flaky: They stop working for no reason and always in the middle of the night. But the problems were familiar. Jiggle the connection, change the board, patch the bug, and restart the system.

In the last 10 years, two new players have come to dominate the workloads and nightmares of the old-style IT type: end users and information.

End users are regular people who just expect their computers to work. They don't know what's inside and they don't want to know. They love "Plug and Play" and scoff at IT's most useful retort: RTFM (Read the F%^&!$# Manual). Manuals are a thing of the past. Users want action, not words.

Information used to just be data. It usually behaved, and if it didn't, that was someone else's problem. Clerks input data and out came reports. Today, end users want to input all sorts of whacky information, and they want it to return as Web pages and all manner of fancy output. Somehow, it is IT's problem to bend systems to meet the unreasonable expectations of end users and their outlandish needs for information presentation.

To represent as clearly as possible the dilemma IT leaders find themselves in, I begin this book in a rather unorthodox way: with a parable, a "historical fiction" that explores the technological, organizational, and human dimensions of the problems that IT professionals confront daily.

We are at a strange point in the development of IT. Information and end users need to be at center stage, but they are still waiting in the wings. You can't fully understand how we got to this point, or more importantly, what we should do now, without first understanding the people involved. Boards, executives, IT leaders, IT staff, and outside product and service providers all have an attitude, an agenda, and a set of expectations of what IT should be. As much as any strategies, tactics, or technologies, their attitudes and interactions drive the development of systems. Like it or not, people really matter.

I will discuss these organizational players throughout the book, but I'd like to introduce them to you in the way, perhaps, that you are most used to seeing them: as the people you work with, trying hard to do a good job but continually banging up against each other's limitations.

In the story that follows, Les Knowles is living the transition from the old IT way to the new. If he were 10 years older, he would probably just wait for retirement. If he were 10 years younger, someone else would have done the hard work for him. In the tale I tell, our hero takes the information bull by the horns. He may or may not be able to subdue it, but at least he has found the right beast. The people in this story are composites of the people I have worked with over the years. I'm hoping that they are enough like the people you work with that you can learn from them. Remember though, this story is simply a prelude to the real story of how you will subdue your own information beast.

Chapters in This Part

Chapter 1: Rebooting IT – Les Knowles begins his tenure as CIO filled with a sense of enthusiasm and promise.

Chapter 2: Information Initiatives – Les tackles the challenges of the information systems his company thinks it needs.

Chapter 3: The Grand Flop – Les sees his grand plan and the very foundation of his position crumble away.

Chapter 4: Strategy Upgrade – Les takes a big step back and considers again what a CIO should do.

Chapter 1

Rebooting IT

Les Knowles, a thin man more comfortable in jeans than in the business suit he was wearing, was sure the CIO job was his. CEO Garrick Pulaski, who had not worn jeans since his waist passed 40, sat behind his desk and smiled. Les had interviewed up and down the corporate ladder and had given all the right answers.

"You would do a good job here," Garrick said. "I like your creativity." But before making an offer, Garrick turned the conversation to Jack Tarr, the outgoing CIO.

"We've decided to make him CTO despite the fact that he is ill equipped to deal with the last 10 years of technology," Garrick said, studying Les' reaction. Les offered a noncommittal nod.

All the new stuff—intranets, communities of practice, wikis, blogs, knowledge management—was beyond Jack's command. The old CIO had paid no attention to these systems. Neither had the CEO nor his executive staff.

"The new CIO will," Les thought.

He wanted this job. He belonged at the executive level. But why were they going to make Jack Tarr CTO?

Garrick said that Jack was an employee of more than 30 years; he had saved the company from technological nightmares many times. He was a friend of the founder and a near god in the eyes of many analysts. And while his programs were slowly being replaced by commercial software, Jack still held the keys to many of the systems that made Allied Financial Services, Inc. (AFS) run. But across AFS, Jack's department was seen as a black hole; support was nonexistent. Most people were using out-of-date software. Sharing information was a nightmare of incompatible and lost files.

"I was brought in to take the business national," Garrick said. "That means expansion, and expansion means leveraging the knowledge of the professional staff across a growing group of new hires."

CTO Jack Tarr

♦ Born 1945 in Columbus, Ohio

♦ BA in Mathematics, CPA

Jack began at AFS as a newly minted CPA in 1966. While he did well as a financial counselor, his passion was the mathematics of finance. He became known as "the numbers guy." As business began to automate in the 1970s, Jack connected AFS to the financial systems that were coming online. He learned programming and hardware support on the job and always kept AFS one step ahead of the larger firms. By 1980, Jack was Director of Computer Services and had a staff of five working on custom applications. When computers moved to desktops, Jack's staff doubled but his interest did not. He cared little for desktop support and GUIs, preferring "real" programs—the ones that did mathematical financial analysis, required an expert to run, and produced reams of tabular output.

"I think we talked before about the chairman's philosophy," said Garrick. Les had heard it from just about everyone who interviewed him. The founder had built the company on the strength of his personal relationships with customers and had handpicked a professional staff that could do the same. Les wondered whether this "founding myth" had become little more than a marketing message.

There was a lot of work needed to get the more recent staff behind that philosophy. Few were naturally able to convert customers into friends. It would be great to apprentice them to the veterans, but most of the old guard worked at AFS headquarters in Columbus, and the new hires were dispersed in offices around the U.S. Plus, the older staff was getting older. Many were reaching retirement, and few wanted to relocate to where they were needed most. In a year or two, Garrick felt the organization would hit a growth wall from a lack of seasoned staff.

Knowledge management was the problem. Jack could not manage to get the knowledge out of the heads of the old guard and decrease training time for employees fresh from college or competing firms.

"So we need to keep Jack, but we need you to go where Jack can't." Jack would be made Chief Technical Officer (CTO), a lateral move. He would oversee the development (or the slow decay) of his analysis systems.

Technically, Les would be his peer as Chief Information Officer (CIO), but Les would be in charge of almost all computer systems.

Les was not entirely happy to have a peer CTO, but he got the picture. He had met many Jacks in his travels and knew that they really did prefer the programmer's cave to the bright lights of the meeting room. Some days, Les too longed for the solitude and creativity of the technologist's life. But that was not the track he was on. Jack would probably be more than happy to give up most of his staff and spend full time on the care and feeding of his Pascal programs.

Les managed to say confidently that it would all be OK, and the talk turned to compensation.

Starting Up

By the spring 2004 board meeting, Les would need to have a staff and a strategic plan in place. His priorities were clear: provide better desktop support for the employees, get the marketing systems going, and "do" knowledge management on a corporate intranet.

The first was a no-brainer. He could hire someone for end-user support. The marketing work was tough, but he had done enterprise systems before and knew the challenges. He had industry contacts and a grasp of the product market. A good Web site for marketing was mostly a matter of getting the right staff and vendors in place.

Knowledge management, on the other hand, seemed vague and ill-conceived. Moving the knowledge of the old-timers into the heads of the newcomers was a noble goal, but Les had no idea how to accomplish this with the computers, databases, and applications that were his stock and trade. Maybe if he could turn up the right products, he could make it happen.

Les organized his staff into three groups:

- **The Desktop and Server group** would ensure that the hardware, software, and support infrastructure was in place, create a standard computer desktop, and establish a help desk.

- **The Enterprise Information Systems group** would own and operate the critical data systems that kept the company running, aside from Jack's analysis programs.

- **The Web Services group** would handle the Web sites and knowledge management applications.

His first job was reorganization. The desktop and server group just needed a strong manager to make sure they did their jobs. But most of the other staff would have to go. They were neither trained nor motivated to do the work that Les had in mind.

The reorganization hit a bump when Jack lobbied Les to help his friends keep their jobs. Les took this as a test of his authority. He flatly refused, and Jack backed off. Les hired a new director for the Desktop and Server group and gave him the best of the old support staff. He decided to manage the Enterprise Systems group himself at first and hired a mix of fresh talent and former colleagues. To lead the Web Services group, he hired Tira Sing, whom he knew to be sharp, trustworthy, and personable. He would leave Tira to build her own team.

At the spring board meeting, Les had a compelling strategy put together and had his key staff positions filled. While he fudged a bit on knowledge management, he was confident that portals, knowledge management systems, and other collaboration applications could be procured and combined into a workable intranet. Neither Garrick nor the board had substantive complaints or changes. They mostly asked about how the re-org had gone and how much his plan would cost. The board and his boss were off his critical path, and he could set his mind toward building systems.

Planning with Sandi

Les was not looking forward to his meeting with Sandra Rodriguez. Pretty and hyper-confident, she reminded him of the girls he could never talk to in high school. And she was not happy. She and Jack had been at loggerheads. Jack gave great service to the analysts, she said, but had no time for marketing. Her CRM system never seemed to make it onto his schedule. Jack's "pocket protector" staff was so "Web-clueless" that she had considered hiring her own Web staff.

Sandra had been abundantly clear about this when she interviewed Les. She had been clear about it a few more times since. Les had heard that she supported his candidacy but was not sure why.

Sandra described her re-org (or "dead wood removal"). After substantial bloodletting, she had brought together business intelligence, media relations, marketing, and sales professionals into a focused group. They had been able to go from market opportunities to branded products in two months.

AFS had grown by an order of magnitude during her watch. Customers were flocking in, and the business was in full swing.

"The problem is we are stretched to the limit. Our analyst staff cannot handle the volume of new customers, and satisfaction is going to fall if the old-guard doesn't start teaching the newcomers how to relate to the customer."

CMO Sandra Rodriguez

◆ Born 1960 in Seattle, Washington

◆ BA in Marketing, MBA

Sandra held many marketing positions in retail before coming to AFS. Her passion has always been for new marketing initiatives that expand customer base. During a campaign aimed at selling paper to financial services institutions, she encountered future AFS CEO Garrick Pulaski. Garrick was impressed with her at the time. In the last few years, she rose within a consumer electronics retailer to the level of Marketing Director. Based on her leadership in the move to take the chain national, Garrick hired her away from the retailer with a promotion to CMO and a substantial pay raise.

"And," she added, "that Web site is a mess. I'm behind you, Les, but you gotta help me here."

She told him to call her Sandi, but she remained Sandra to him as they planned out the approach to her CRM system and Web site.

Web Services

By the time Les had returned from the spring board meeting, Tira was already settled in and down to business. She had cut her long black hair to "director length" and pushed her jeans and saris aside for a new flock of business suits.

Tira had helped Les prepare the board presentation, so she was no stranger to what it proposed. Together, they boiled her major initiatives down to a new Web site for the marketing group and a "next generation" intranet that did knowledge management and collaboration.

After a month of review, the plan was approved as Tira had drafted it. With her team in place, she was set for a summer launch of the new Web site and a winter launch of the intranet. Les had lobbied to cut these schedules in half, but Tira held firm, having been burned in the past by an executive's unrealistic timeline.

The other directors had also delivered realistic and fundable plans. Les began the fall season confident that he and his team would reinvent IT at AFS.

Chapter 2

Information Initiatives

Les figured that marketing was the key to his success. Marketing was the new, cool group everyone was looking to and also his biggest client. So he made the marketing group's CRM application his top priority.

The CRM Application

The CRM application, Sandra said, would enable a personal approach to each customer. A personal approach, in turn, would require that records of all interactions be available to anyone with customer contact. The idea was pretty standard: Know your customer. But now it was the computer that was supposed to know. With the thousands of customers who didn't know what they wanted and the constant throughput of sales and support people, technology was the only hope of maintaining relationships.

Les' business analyst reported back after a month. "Aside from some generalities about relationships, horror stories about certain CRM systems, and pleas for particular vendors, no one had much to say. If this is the big deal that they insist it is, you'd think they would have more interest in figuring it out."

"Typical," commiserated Les. "But how different can each of these systems be?"

The analyst suggested that AFS invite a few vendors to come in and demo. Les agreed, though he knew it was not wise to have vendors set requirements. As he expected, each company seemed better than the last. They all had great features, well-known customers, and assuring answers to every question. The staff's apathy seemed to disappear. People took notes and argued over products. After five demos, Sandra's group was buzzing with feature requests. The analyst boiled them down to a number of "must-haves." Les thought that they were more "would be cool to haves" but told the analyst to proceed anyway.

While the analyst transformed the requirements into a Request for Proposal (RFP), marketing was performing its own selection process fueled by the relationships that the product companies had managed to form at the demos.

"They let the vendors lead them by the nose," Les thought. "You'd think our marketers would be wise to their own tricks." Still, the demos had resuscitated the process and engaged the client. At least the marketing group was getting educated on CRM.

Les stepped in to lead the final selection knowing that it could get hot. Despite his best attempts, it turned into a horse race. People ignored his spreadsheets and cheered on their favorite vendors. So Les left the haggling to the marketing group and confined himself to making sure that whatever they chose was technically sound, compatible with their existing platforms, and not too much work to implement.

At last, the group managed to choose a product that everyone could live with. A contract was signed and installation began. The application was harder to get running than Les expected, but they stayed close to schedule.

The customization of the product was another story. More than once, Les had lived through implementations driven by a kaleidoscope of ill-conceived feature requests. To avoid that nightmare, he insisted that the technical staff write specifications of how the features would be implemented. But when the business analyst tried to engage the marketing group, he found that their apathy had returned. The group seemed to feel that its work was done.

Les told Sandra that if she wanted a successful implementation, she needed to get her staff involved again.

"Les, choosing a vendor already strained my team. We told you what we want. Can't you just make it do that?"

"No," he said flatly. "This is not our system; it is yours. If you can't put the time in to make it work, maybe it is not worth doing."

It was a statement of fact, but to Sandra, it sounded more like a threat.

"OK," she said in a business formal tone. "You tell me what resources you need, and I will tell you what I can spare."

Sandra left the room with a smile, but Les was unsure whether the meeting had gone well. He had gotten what he wanted, but she didn't seem altogether happy. In fact, she wasn't, and she told her staff so. If the staff wanted software, the staff would have to "play the IT game and probably start filling out forms."

It took more than three weeks to put together a meeting between the project team and marketing. Les outlined a plan calling for participation from two analysts, one system administrator, one training supervisor, and one documentation specialist from Sandra's team. It also called for review and acceptance of the specification from Sandra and her directors.

When the business analyst recommended that changes go through "the standard change form process," a chuckle issued from marketing. The marketing group accepted its responsibilities as outlined, even if the group did assign the same person to most of the jobs. The project could now move forward, but Les suspected that the problems were not over.

By the end of 2004, the CRM system was ready to be launched. Its features were fewer than what had been in the RFP, but it seemed to have the big things that the marketing group had asked for.

The Web Site

Tira began work as soon she had hired her team and secured her budget. She reported to Les that the current external site was a mid-1990s design with a lot of old content. She laid out the enhancements that would bring the site up-to-date technologically. Les pushed for a simple update first.

"Let's improve the look and feel," he said, "and kill the out-of-date content. We can roll out more advanced features later. For now, let's establish our reputation for quick turnaround of good-looking sites."

During the next few months, the project team met with people in marketing and found, to no one's surprise, that marketing was short on time and requirements and long on desires. The IT team never got to meet actual end users and was told summarily that whatever content was on the site now was pretty much what should be there. Later on, however, the IT team got more content ideas than it knew what to do with. They began to receive emails with attachments, directory locations, and vague recommendations.

These emails landed on the desk of Allena Nhlahla, the newly hired information architect and Web designer. When Tira asked about the emails, Allena expressed her frustration and then pointed out a more serious problem. Only about half of the material on the site was from marketing. The other half was from just about every other group in the company. The marketing half was fairly well organized, while the rest seemed scattered and of dubious value. She offered to do a fuller audit of the information that each group needed on the site and modify its structure accordingly.

"Can of worms," Tira thought. Redefining the site now could dilute its focus and upset marketing—her main (and as far as she knew only) client. She asked Allena to choose a sample of the nonmarketing pages and find out how much they were used. Allena soon reported back that the server logs were never completely configured, but from what she could infer, most of the pages in question were low in popularity. Some of them had only been accessed once or twice.

Web Services Director Tira Sing

- ◆ Born 1965 in Bangalore, India

- ◆ MS in Computer Science

Tira began as a programmer in the IT department of a software development firm. She soon switched to network administration where she climbed quickly up the IT ranks, first with the software company and then, after that company folded, with the same financial services company where Les had worked. She left to become IT Director in an e-commerce dot-com. There she kept the e-commerce system healthy and running. Within a year, however, the dot-com went under, and through her contact with Les she got the job at AFS.

Tira figured that this was more than enough information to make a decision herself, but she checked with Les anyway.

In their weekly meeting, she asked if anyone else had come forward with requirements for the site besides marketing.

"I've never heard anyone but marketing even mention it," replied Les.

"We have lots of pages from other groups," Tira said. "Nobody seems to own them and some have hardly ever been accessed. Is it OK to get rid of them?"

Something Les had read came back to him.

"Web sites are saddled with layers of stuff hanging on for no good reason. Let's trim that dead wood and see what happens. If anyone complains, we can put pages back up, but I bet no one will."

Tira told Allena to cut the nonmarketing pages from the site. Allena seemed hesitant.

"Listen," Tira said, "you looked at the logs. Those pages are dead. And this is straight from the CIO. He said to lose the nonmarketing stuff."

"Whatever," said Allena, rolling her eyes. Everyone knew the CIO was clueless. Tira pursed her lips. She looked Allena up and down, regarding her artsy vintage outfit. She was not impressed.

Allena realized she had transgressed. She asked Tira politely what she should do about all the ideas that were flooding her inbox. When Tira suggested that

Allena have some meetings with marketing, Allena barely resisted rolling her eyes again. Everyone knew that marketing was clueless too.

Just another messed up company ...

Allena just shrugged. It was all too familiar—the lack of executive support, the unresponsive clients, the "go-it-alone" mentality, and the over-reliance on technology—all of it boded ill for this IT group. She couldn't quit this soon, but how much longer could she stay?

They were well into the spring when Tira stopped trying to collaborate with marketing. To have any hope of a summer launch, her group would need to take what they had and start building. The decision met no resistance.

At Allena's suggestion, Tira agreed to warn marketing once more that without help the site content would suffer. Tira passed this message unfiltered to Les who took it to Sandra. Their relationship had chilled since their disagreements over the CRM system.

"We tried to help those Web people," Sandra said, "but they could never say clearly what they wanted. They talk about a Web site that will be ready in six months but can't help us with what we need to get on the site today."

"In fact," she added, "while your team builds our future Web site, maybe we should take over the current one and hire a vendor to get our critical pages on it."

Les rejected the idea immediately. He instead suggested that the marketing team hold a meeting with the IT group to discuss their differences. The meeting never materialized, so the Web team stopped analyzing and started building.

Feelings warmed somewhat when the prototype was unveiled. Allena had done outstanding work on the look and feel, which is what marketing paid the most attention to, and she had helped the writer put together a sensible content outline. Tensions eased all the way up the ladder and, for a time, Les felt that he was out of the woods with Sandra.

Around the time of the originally scheduled launch, the Web team began building in earnest. The writer and a contractor fashioned the content while the programmers began building pages. By early winter, AFS had a beautiful new marketing Web site.

The Intranet

With the troubles elsewhere, the intranet and its knowledge management had fallen behind schedule. Les and Tira decided to tackle the problem together. Tira began by surveying the existing intranet sites.

"It's a mess. There's no way to know how many intranet sites we have, let alone how good their information is. Anyone who read 'HTML in 24 Hours' has a site, and every site has its own look and feel, if you can call it that. It's out of control."

Les was surprised that so many people at AFS were into the Web, but he filed that idea for the moment and offered that they should declare a moratorium on new intranet pages until the existing ones could at least be cataloged and accounted for.

"This will meet resistance," Tira countered. "People like their little creations. They love to mess around with technology they don't understand."

Les took the issue to the CEO. Garrick had not even known about the intranet sites. He was pleased that people had made the effort, but he agreed to issue the memo to stop work on unofficial sites pending the launch of the official site.

Garrick, Les, and Tira were blindsided by the response to Garrick's memo. Emails poured in immediately stating how important these sites were—people reasoned, pleaded, and threatened on their behalf. One young analyst in the new California office even quit, citing the "draconian decrees from the Midwest." Les was called back to the office of an unhappy Garrick, where he tried to explain away the response as vanity and pride.

He repeated Tira's phrase, "people like their little creations," but Garrick would have none of it.

"Some might be playing," Garrick said, "but not all of them. I can't believe that you didn't anticipate this. This is a PR disaster. I'm going to have to rescind the memo and apologize. You're going to have to find a way to work with these people rather than against them."

Les had no idea how to work with these people or even who they were, but he was in no position to say so. Deflated and confused, he called Tira into his office. She maintained that the reaction had more to do with the pride than with any real value that the sites were providing.

"Be that as it may," chided Les, "the situation has changed. We have to take these people seriously and figure out how to manage them without shutting them down. Got any ideas?"

They decided that version one of the intranet would not encompass the existing sites. It would focus on new features that were of enterprise significance, like knowledge management. They would hire a consulting company to inventory the existing sites so that the next time they decided to shut down a renegade site, they would have evidence of its lack of value.

Garrick issued the apology: "Given the importance of your intranet sites to our success, we will initiate a thorough analysis of your current uses of the Web and figure out how to pull it all together."

The extra money for this initiative came so easily that Tira joked to her staff that they had discovered a new funding technique.

Knowledge Central

The intranet had to "do" knowledge management. Les knew there was a problem training new people, but he was not sure what exactly it was or how to address it.

Tira unearthed some material created by company founder Wilbur Evans. During the coming expansion, Wilbur wrote, the key to success would be to extend the values of quick response and personal customer relationships as the company grew.

Les and Tira white-boarded a system where new folks could find mentors and old folks could hold court in blogs and discussion groups. Tira looked for users to interview. She located a few newcomers in the expansion offices and went down the hall to find an old-timer or two. After a week of email tag, she turned up some useful information.

An old-timer close to retirement rhapsodized about the days when Wilbur managed the company by hand. He doubted that the attitude he inspired could be replaced by a computer, but he thought that better communication with the new offices would be good nonetheless. He suggested that Wilbur be given a platform on the new system.

A more incisive veteran recalled the rise of IT inside AFS and the tensions between the new marketing and the old IT group. He hoped that Les' group would do better though he candidly doubted that they would. The idea of mentoring was farfetched without personal contact but good. He suggested that rather than spend money on computers they hold a retreat where the new and old staff could get to know each other. He said that the old staff might not be able or willing to record their knowledge, but if they would, there would be a lot to write. Finally, he said they would not get excited easily. They had been holding the company together for years now, preserving the original vision but seeing it cheapened by marketing for the sake of expansion.

Les tried to sort out the requirements from the folklore. The old-timers had not disagreed with the idea; they were just cynical. And as one of them said, "If it is done really well, people might use it."

When Tira talked to new analysts and support staff in the remote offices, she learned immediately that they did not like being called "remote." They reminded her that the market was larger outside of Ohio than within it. And they did not necessarily want to learn from the old guard. They liked the idea of quick response and personal relationships, but they had their own ideas about what it meant.

"For one thing," one of them said, "there are tools I use on the Web now that some of the older staff have only dreamed of."

Still, they all believed that they should be in better contact with their peers in the central office, and a few even said that they would love to have a mentor.

For the first time, it occurred to Les that the whole idea of knowledge transfer might be a bit off. Maybe it was the right move a few years back, but was it now? The old guard was aging and outnumbered; the new guard was arrogant and unconvinced that there was life before the Web. He expressed this to Tira.

"We've got a great idea." She replied, "And if it is good, they will use it."

With a bit of creative extrapolation, they solidified the intranet's knowledge management features:

- **Expertise locator** where the old guard specifies their expertise and new staff search the profiles and documents for topic-related terms

- **Discussion threads** on topics moderated by the old-timers

- **Blogs** where experts issue opinions on key topics

- **Knowledge repository** where people could share job-critical files

Tira was assigned to find software while Les enlisted participants. Starting at the top, he invited the founder Wilbur Evans to have a blog, explaining that a blog was like a public journal. He could write whatever needed to be said, and people could respond. Wilbur immediately grasped that this was a way he could reassert his presence in the company. Les was relieved to have at least one star in the system.

Meanwhile, Tira found a company that could meet the requirements and do the implementation quickly. Les jumped at the chance to show that IT could be decisive and creative. Soon there was a working installation and a demo of all the proposed features. When the rest of the intranet was completed, "Knowledge Central" could be integrated with it.

The product vendor insisted that the success of its system lay not in its features but in its adoption. Les and Tira, the company observed, had pushed out ahead of the rest of the organization. The vendor argued that a great knowledge-sharing system with nobody using it was worse than no system at all.

The product company suggested that Les do an internal marketing campaign to put knowledge transfer at the front of people's minds. The celebrity contributors plus the marketing campaign would get people engaged. The engaged people would reach critical mass and drive adoption throughout AFS. The system could then move forward without much IT presence. There was a lot of work to be done to moderate the forums, provide vocabularies for the text-mining and file-sharing software, and seed the system with documents of value to users. All this would have to be started by IT and then transitioned to the users.

Tira stole what time she could from Allena to create posters, leaflets, Web pages, and emails announcing and extolling Knowledge Central. Allena thought Tira was joking at first and giggled. Had Allena's work not been so good, Tira would have fired "Miss Second-Hand Store" on the spot. A few days later, Allena's request to extend her year-end break was denied. Allena responded by posting a resume on Monster.com.

Chapter 3

The Grand Flop

The new year rolled in with things pretty much under control for Les Knowles. The CRM system was ready to go, as were the external site and a big piece of the intranet. Desktops were more standardized, and the servers had never been so robust. There had been trouble, but no more than was reasonable.

But things did not look so good from other perspectives within AFS. The marketing group, spurred by Sandra's open cynicism, had all but written off IT. The group liked the new Web site, but it did not want to repeat such a painful process. CRM had promise but mostly because the marketing group had chosen a good system. IT had done a lot of posturing but had not brought much value to the table.

CIO Les Knowles

- Born 1955 in Atlanta, Georgia

- BS in Electrical Engineering, MBA

Les followed the track of many of the technically astute of the baby boom generation: engineering. Les graduated near the top of his class and excelled as a pioneering electronics design manager. Later, in his elite MBA program, he learned management, finance, accounting, and marketing. He was left on his own to figure out how these related to technology, and he did it well enough to continually distinguish himself. He rose through the ranks of IT management and finally landed a director job in a financial services firm. His success there got him the CIO job at AFS.

Outside of marketing, in offices all over the U.S., tech-savvy analysts, unofficial Webmasters, and a host of other digerati had gotten the message that the central office was clamping down. The first attempt was repulsed, but they were not fooled. They knew that another attempt to rein them in would follow on the heels of the "analysis initiative." Les' attempts to enforce a standard desktop put people on edge as they lost more and more control over their own computers.

The Digerati Rebel

In mid-January, Tira threw the switch, and the new marketing site replaced the old. The digerati gasped. The same staff that had been creating intranets had also been posting to the external site for years.

The Web is freedom ...

For Jack Tarr, the old CIO, the Web was the ultimate self-expression tool. Anyone could own a piece of the AFS site, which consequently became a microcosm of the Web itself: a touch of brilliance mixed with large shares of mediocrity, redundancy, and trash. Almost all of this abundance was hidden from public view because it was not included in the site navigation. Publishers would distribute URLs via email to their constituents within and outside AFS.

Most of these sites fell into disuse. Some, however, boasted a small but committed set of contributors and users sharing information. When Tira shut off the old site, the owners of these "going concerns" noticed immediately and demanded recourse.

Les found himself again in the office of a disturbed CEO.

"Les, what the hell is this? I thought you handled this thing a long time ago." He turned his screen toward Les and showed him an email from a manager in Baltimore.

Shaken, Les scanned the screen and saw: "... IT shut us off ...," "... site critical to our business ...," and "... not consulted."

It must be a mistake. They had not shut down any intranets. He looked again and saw, "... use the Web site to work with customers ..." It wasn't the intranet that they were upset about; it was the new marketing site.

He had forgotten the "shut them down and see who complains" conversation with Tira months ago. Under Garrick's hard gaze, he fumbled to reconstruct his logic.

Garrick interrupted. "This is not the only one I've gotten. Why did you shut off the intranet?"

"It's not the intranet," Les began. "It's the marketing site. We found thousands of unused and inaccessible pages on it. Only marketing gave us requirements. Jack let the site get out of control," he added. "Anyone could post to it. We had no indication of who these pages belonged to." He inhaled, hoping he had turned the tone of the conversation.

Garrick figured he got the thrust.

"So after the trouble we had with the intranet, you did the same thing with the other one."

"Before. It was actually before the intranet. That's why I forgot." Les immediately wished he hadn't said "forgot." He continued: "If it had been after, I would have done it differently."

"You forgot," said Garrick slowly, "and you didn't think to go looking further than the marketing department, even though you found all sorts of non-marketing stuff on the site?" Les did not respond.

Garrick moderated his tone. "Look, Les, before this job you were an IT director, right?" Les nodded and felt the cut before it was delivered.

"The job of a director is to carry out policy. The job of a chief is to make policy. I know Jack left you a hell of a mess. You've had a year to turn that around. Year one you get the benefit of the doubt. Year two, the burden is on you. Get ahead of this, Les. I need you to lead, man."

Les left with his head down. Why hadn't he seen this coming? If someone besides Garrick had told him, he could have gone on the offensive. He quickened his pace toward Tira's office.

Tira did not admit her part in the fiasco. In fact, she still seemed to feel that they had been right.

"The ones who complained can still have their pages reinstated. Good riddance to the rest."

Les recognized his own words coming back at him and felt sick at their arrogance. He saw the digerati's point of view. They were making serious use of the Web, and he was in their way.

"You would be the first to complain if you were out there in a remote office," he snapped. Tira bowed her head and scowled.

Les sent apologies to all the people who had complained and included this appeal: "We would appreciate a third strike before you call us out. We intend to take your Web efforts most seriously in the future."

Tira reluctantly restored the old pages. Les pulled together some more money to pay the consultants to sort out the mess.

The digerati were not feeling particularly forgiving. They could sense Les' humility, but so what? They curtailed the open rebellion and contented themselves with circulating IT jokes:

> *Q: How many IT geeks does it take to change a light bulb?*
> *A: Only one, but she's not available till the year 2010.*

> *Q: How many IT geeks does it take to change a light bulb?*
> *A: Well, we have an exact copy of your light bulb here and it seems to be working OK. Can you be more specific about the problem?*

> *Q: How many IT geeks does it take to change a light bulb?*
> *A: We looked at the light fixture and decided there's no point trying to maintain it. We're going to rewrite it from scratch. Could you wait two months?*

With the crisis stemmed, Les found space for a bit of perspective. "So," he said at the next staff meeting, "we got mail from about 10 owners who account for about 200 of the 3,000 nonmarketing pages. Our failed policy actually succeeded 92.5 percent of the time."

Knowledge Central Tanks

When the AFS staff returned to work in 2005, they were greeted with announcements of Knowledge Central:

> *"Dump your brain and expand your mind."*
> *"Learn from the experts, teach the customer."*
> *"When we know what we know, you will find it on Knowledge Central."*

Those who were enticed by the posters found the same sloganeering on the home page accompanied by links to Discussions, Knowledge Repository, Expert Central, and Blogs, each of which opened an attractive page with more slogans, buttons, lists, and calls for user participation. Tira had seeded the site with enough content to show how it worked but not nearly enough to suggest that it had much of a constituency.

A few people took up the challenge, starting discussions and waiting for responses. After a week, two dozen .doc and .ppt files appeared in the Knowledge Repository, awkwardly displayed because of improperly completed upload forms. Six new experts joined the initial seven. One was listed as an "Annuities Expert Expert" and another as a "Lifetime Expert."

The blogs page featured a bio of Wilbur followed by profiles of the other contributors. While most had written perfunctory "Welcome to My Journal" overtures, Wilbur led with a fiery invective, challenging the old and new to realize the ideal of quick response. The old guard had the experience but not the energy, while the young Turks had the savvy but not the seasoning.

Wilbur's blog generated just the stir Les hoped it would, but its cache did not spread to the rest of Knowledge Central. The popularity of the other pages peaked in the second week and then fell off sharply.

You call that knowledge?

After two months, there were only 10 discussions; the longest had five entries. Of 56 "knowledge items," 20 of them were posted by the same person and only a handful had been downloaded. Four of 24 experts had quit because of bothersome emails from people looking for advice. "What did they expect?" Les thought.

Wilbur's blog flourished. The other bloggers had taken Wilbur's lead and staked positions relative to his. People posted lengthy spell-checked responses. Requests for new blogs flowed in. There was just one problem: The logs showed that AFS was bypassing the Knowledge Central home page and flocking directly to Wilbur's page.

Les called Wilbur to thank him and ask him to promote the rest of Knowledge Central. Wilbur just chuckled and said, "Sorry, I have bigger fish to fry." As participation fell even more, Les considered quietly shutting down Knowledge Central. But, still feeling the sting of the incidents with the digerati, he decided to leave well enough alone.

The flop did not go unnoticed, however, and the email jokes spread. Someone scanned Tira's ads and changed the slogans:

> *"Dump the IT group and expand your budget."*
> *"If we only knew what they were doing, we could stop them."*

When Les got wind of this, he told Tira to give the blogs page its own URL and take down Knowledge Central. Tira argued that if they could just get Wilbur and the others to go to bat for them, the site would take off. The two of them fought more vehemently than ever. Finally, Les told Tira it was a dead idea and to just forget it and move on.

Marketing Defects

Les was unaware of the animosity IT had aroused in marketing until he tried to turn over the keys to the CRM system. He had been warned that they were not ready to own the application, but he decided to force the issue. He told the project manager to send an email to the person Sandra had assigned to be the system administrator, trainer, documenter, and analyst. The "do it all" person was pleasant enough but was unskilled and only half-interested in the CRM tasks. He would never say that he didn't understand, but he never quite did.

Within the hour, Sandra was in Les' office as Les had anticipated. Before she could begin, he raised his finger aloft, a gesture intended to say both "I understand" and "Please, no undue emotion." Sandra's eyes narrowed, and she stopped speaking.

"I know you are in a tough position. But the project plan, which you okayed, specified that you would assume all maintenance by now. I understand that you're not quite ready. But I hope you understand that we cannot run your application for you. However, we can support you for the next couple of months while you beef up your staff."

Stunned for a moment, Sandra forced a smile.

"No, you're right, Les. I'm sorry we have to depend on you longer than planned. If you continue to support us through this month, I promise that we'll take it from there." She turned briskly and left.

Les involuntarily let out a small involuntary hoot. He had played it perfectly—defused her anger, gotten her to see she was wrong, and even persuaded her to take full responsibility. Sandra heard that hoot and flashed fury in Les' direction as she walked away.

There were some earnest CRM users who tried to replace their manual customer contact procedures with the new system. But as the second month of support wore on, it became clear to IT and marketing alike that they had only scratched the surface of the problem. They had not even moved past the question of what a "customer" or a "relationship" were. Their sales process was totally different from what IT had assumed. They argued at length about whether to change the system to match their process or change their process to match the system.

IT balked at the work it would take to change the system, reminding marketing that if they had engaged when they were supposed to, they could be using the system by now. Marketing, in turn, treated IT as if it was an unnecessary burden. "You just don't get what we are trying to do," marketing repeated, and "can't you just make it do ...?"

After six weeks, Les was ready to confront Sandra. She seemed no more prepared to take over than when she last walked out of his office. Then marketing went silent; the department stopped returning email and attending meetings.

When Les emailed Sandra, she replied in one sentence.

"Thanks for the help, Les, but we won't be needing it anymore."

This time it was Les in Sandra's office. And this time, it was Sandra who preempted Les with a raised finger.

"Is she mocking me?" he thought.

"That was good advice you gave me, Les," she began. "We need to take ownership, so I've engaged a consulting firm to help us with the CRM system. Garrick approved it. They are really great. They'll take the burden of support right off of your team."

"Actually," Les said, "we are happy to support you. We just want you to own ..."

"Absolutely. We will own it all. So if you can have your team send over all of the work we've done to date, we'll just take it from here."

This was not turning out right. Why had she gone outside AFS? Why hadn't she at least asked his opinion? Was this OK?

"Thanks, Les," Sandra said.

A few feet down the hall, he heard a distinct hoot.

His eyes watered slightly as he thought, "She *is* mocking me."

Les walked half way to Garrick's office before losing his nerve. She said he had approved it all.

The End Draws Near

The spring board meeting was two weeks away, and Les would need to report on his initiatives. He pulled out his scorecard. He was within budget. He had staffed up and had standardized the server platform. The data center was in great shape, and there had been no server outages for more than six months—all plusses. But then, there was the other stuff, the stuff that really mattered.

He was supposed to bring the IT directors of the regional offices under his supervision, but they had sided with the digerati, so he was waiting before exerting control. Next, there was the bloody struggle that ensued to standardize the desktops. Even in the main office, he met with dissent. In the remote locations, there was rampant passive resistance. The ire was mostly aimed at his director, but he could claim no victories.

The Web site had launched, yes, but little credit had come to his team. After pulling CRM from him, Sandra had yanked "her" Web site too. Garrick had approved that as well.

He would have to avoid Knowledge Central entirely, but he could point to the blogs, which were the talk of the company. His group came up with the idea. His people were the administrators. So why did everyone equate the blogs with Wilbur Evans, as if he needed more recognition?

All in all, it was a pretty poor performance. He considered quitting before the meeting. Maybe he wasn't cut out for CIO. As a director, he was always ahead of his bosses and received praise at every turn. Here, the harder he tried to "get in front of the issues and lead," the more trouble he caused. No one considered him a leader. He was the "Chief Incompetence Officer" heading for a "Career In Obscurity."

A week before the board meeting, Garrick invited Les out to dinner. "Good time to quit," he thought, "before Garrick has a chance to fire me."

When the small talk had been exhausted, Garrick began.

CEO Garrick Pulaski

- Born 1950 in Chicago, Illinois

- BA in Finance, MBA

Garrick has held just about every position possible within an investment firm. He worked his way through the management ranks in various institutions to become CFO in his last firm. Known to be hard-nosed and practical but fair, he has a strong understanding and commitment to marketing. Compared to his competitors for the CEO position at AFS, he was seen as the compromise candidate between marketing (the key to growth) and finance (the key to stability).

"Have you thought about how you will present yourself at the board meeting?"

"*Is* there a way to present myself?"

"Look," said Garrick, "you brought that thing with Sandi on yourself. You provided her with all the ammo she needed to go outside."

"What did I ever do to her?"

"I don't know. But I don't think it's personal. She doesn't talk about you, but about IT people, technology types, and bureaucracy."

So he was a stereotype now? "This place is poison," he thought.

"OK, Garrick, I'm done. Can we get me out without too much backwash into the rest of my career? It's not working. I'm gonna look like a fool at the board meeting and I'm gonna hate the satisfaction that will be on Sandi's face when I do."

Garrick looked Les in the eye. "If that's what it is about then I'll be glad to see you go. I got the impression when we hired you that looking good was not what motivated you, that you could find your own way."

What do they know?

Garrick and his knowledge transfer routine. Just so much warmed over lather from something he had heard someone else say. Sandra and her CRM. She had no idea what that meant or how she would have to transform her group in order to do it. "With or without me," Les thought, "they would learn their lessons."

Les began to respond, but Garrick continued.

"This year's initiatives were just your first round. We need to move on soon. We need to get our records in order before that compliance audit. We need full-service sites like the big players. We need to cut staffing costs and increase the speed of transactions. We need a CIO who can tell us what we need to do next and how all that technology can help us. Just convince us that you will pull it together in the future. If nobody buys it, we'll get you out of here with a minimum of pain."

Les was unconvinced. He didn't have a plan for the future. On the other hand, he had been thinking of the board meeting as an evaluation. Seeing it as an opportunity to create a new agenda made him brighten a bit.

"OK," he said. "I'll do my best at the board meeting, and then let's decide."

Chapter 4

Strategy Upgrade

Monday morning at 10 AM, Les' IT group meeting began. The day's agenda included intranet issues and a report from the consultant on the digerati and their Web sites.

Les was not the only one feeling the heat. His team had seen the organization's confidence decline and they had divided into two hostile camps. Tira and about one-third of the professional staff wanted to circle the wagons, forcing other groups to sign off on plans, commit resources, and fill out change forms. The other camp had no spokesperson and no proposal, but it had two-thirds of the professional staff. It argued that IT was not user-centered enough. Staying close to the end user would ensure that IT systems would succeed.

Les did not like either idea. Not 10 minutes into the meeting, with the outside consultant watching, the two sides began to bicker over the intranet.

"Stop!" he barked. "This is a senseless argument! It's obviously possible for us to engage users and have defined processes as well. My god, Tira, if we can't even figure out how to work with ourselves, how will we ever figure out how to work with the rest of the organization?"

A thick silence fell. Yes, exactly. How would they work with the rest of the organization? That was what they all wanted to know and what he should now tell them. Les had an urge to get up and walk out, but the moment passed.

"He's a weak leader and everyone knows it," thought Tira as she shot him daggers.

"Well," Les quickly added, "I'm sure we'll get it straightened out. Maybe we should have the report now on Web usage in the remote offices."

Les melted into his seat and his dark thoughts. He had not read the report and didn't really care what it had to say. Tira introduced the analyst and then retreated into her own funk.

The analyst glanced around at the distracted group and then at his slide projected on the wall. He set his laser pointer down and said: "So, do you want the good news first or the bad?" Heads around the table began to rise.

Noticing that he was supposed to answer, Les replied, "Good, please."

"Great. The good news is actually pretty good." He began talking about an initiative in San Diego. They had managed to create online portfolios. Clients received an unchanging URL where they could monitor all their investments. Graphs illustrated the performance of funds. A few standard links showed how the market as a whole had performed. Analysts could add explanations and advice.

"It's pretty simple," the consultant said, "but everyone there loves it and," he paused, "hopes you won't shut it down. Good things are happening out there. This is far from the only one."

The consultant presented an overview of a couple more "cool sites," and then concluded, "you've got a great set of natural allies out there pulling the organization forward."

"Allies?" Les thought. "Those people are killing me." But then he reconsidered. "So how many of these digerati are there and what are their skills?"

The consultant smiled and said that Les had chosen the right term for them. It was hard to estimate, but there were probably no more than a dozen real drivers supported by a couple of dozen committed resources and maybe 50 or 60 volunteers. Other people began to perk up and ask questions.

Hungry for something good to talk about, they discussed the digerati for nearly an hour. Tira ignored them. During a lull, Les asked what everyone else was afraid to ask. "The bad news?"

"Well," hesitated the consultant, "it's more an opportunity than bad news per se." Silence descended again. "And I think you pretty much know it already. Most of the people I talked to consider your group to be a barrier more than a help. They believe," he hesitated, "that you want to control them. Some have far-fetched conspiracy theories, but most just take the view that their central IT unit is heavy handed, out of touch, and to be avoided."

Survival of the useful ...

"Many pages have low-usage," said the consultant, "but that doesn't mean that they're unimportant. Some are really critical. The sites that are vital enough to warrant the effort live. The others die. It's pretty Darwinian."

All around the table, there was grumbling and blooming anger. Tira inhaled to speak.

"But to be fair," the consultant quickly added, "that's not an unusual attitude. Frankly, it's about the norm. People hate IT on principle; it's nothing personal." He stopped, realizing he had gone over the line. But the words hit Les like a brick: "Not personal … Everyone hates IT."

Tira inhaled again, but Les spoke first. "So we are the stereotypical IT group, are we?" The consultant braced for rebuke until Les looked back at him reassuringly.

"How the hell did it get that way? Does anyone here think of themselves as the 'typical IT jerk'? I sure don't. You know what the typical IT jerk does? He reacts! He never acts. He never tells you what you should be doing, only what you shouldn't or can't."

Everyone absorbed Les' remarks. The consultant broke the silence just before it got uncomfortable.

"So," he said, advancing to the next slide, "we understand your desire to coalesce all of the 'rogue sites' into a single intranet. After all, everyone needs an intranet. But a couple of issues stand in your way. Many of these sites are their own little operations, a combination of intranet, Internet site, and extranet site. There are even printed materials produced in conjunction with some. It's hard to break off the intranet part. Conglomerating them on a new page with a standard header and footer doesn't seem to buy you much at this point."

Les had missed most of this explanation. He had gotten stuck on the phrase "a single intranet." He said almost to himself, "Why do we need a single intranet?" The question suddenly seemed so obvious. Why had he never asked Garrick or the board or Tira or anyone?

The consultant seemed confused by the question, as if there were some trick to it that he wasn't getting.

"I suppose it is more for you to tell me, but most people need an intranet to organize all of their internal facing information and provide a one-stop shop. Intranets centralize information and make it accessible through the convenient medium of the Web."

Allena Nhlahla had been sitting quietly for the entire meeting. She was outranked by just about everyone in the room, but she spoke anyway.

"It seems to me that you just told us that we don't need an intranet. All those people are doing fine without some behemoth of a site that is all things to all people. They had a problem, and they found their own solution, thank you very much. What's the point of us stepping all over that? Isn't that what you're saying?"

"Um, yes and no. Yes, you shouldn't try just yet to smash together all of the internal sites, but no, you should not give up on the idea of an intranet."

Allena countered, "So at what point *is* it OK to smash together all those sites? Why wouldn't we just let them do what they do and leave them alone?"

"Well, at some point, you should be in a position to leverage the investment and information in the individual systems across the whole organization. What if someone wanted to get to the information that is trapped in one of those systems? You might want a global data model that lets anyone reach into any system, and at that point, you have a global intranet and you might as well call it that."

The room seemed to be in agreement with this. Les was looking distract-edly toward Allena, who took this as a cue to stop talking.

Les turned toward the consultants and said, "Thanks so much for the great presentation. I can't remember when we have had so much good discussion. It's usually all logistics and deliverables."

Attitude Hot Swap

Allena was halfway down the hall when Les caught up with her.

"Excuse me," he called. "Hi, uh," he stumbled. "Could you repeat what you said just now to those consultants?" The mistrust in her eyes backed him off.

"I mean," he said, "it sounded right to me, and I don't want to forget it." Allena's initial trepidation washed back. She considered the man in front of her. "Out of touch" came to her mind, then "old school" and then, strangely, "sincere." Like her, he was on his way out. Unlike her, he would rather not be.

"His own evidence led him to a conclusion he was unwilling to make. Why do we need to control all the independent efforts? He could only describe some golden future when all information is accessible and useful to everyone."

She looked hard at Les and then went on.

"The intranet is bullshit. It has no reason to be except that someone said to do it. I've been on it for months, and I have yet to see why we need it." Allena found herself suddenly way outside her comfort zone.

"I'm not saying that we don't need it; I'm just saying that no one has ever told me why we do. Where's the value?"

Les' head told him to set this woman straight. His heart told him that he had just been set straight.

"Strong words," he said. "I don't have anything right now I can't cancel. Can we chat?" Allena had planned to meet with Tira after the staff meeting to announce her search for a new job but that could wait.

"Um, sure."

"So the intranet is bullshit?" he said as they sat in his office.

Web Designer Allena Nhlahla

♦   Born 1961 in Los Alamos, New Mexico

♦   BA in Fine Arts

Raised by a scientist, Allena grew up immersed in his rational pursuits but strained against them. She swore that she would be a fine artist. After college, her practical side emerged. She worked for a technical writing company doing illustrations and layout for print. As computers began to redefine the job of design, Allena devoured every new application, learned the Macintosh operating system, and established her own home network at a time when most companies were still unconnected. An independent consultant for years, she was able to talk to programmers as well as to artists. She took the job at AFS despite her fears that she would be hamstrung by politics. She wanted the stability and benefits but not the headaches.

"Maybe that's an overstatement. What I mean is that we assume that there has to be something called 'The Intranet.' All you have to do populate it with information that people want. But the intranet before the content is like the cart before the horse."

Les agreed. She had completed the thought he had begun in the meeting. "But," he added, "if you don't have an intranet, what do you have?"

"What you have," she said, "are users who need information and suppliers that have information. We also have channels of communication to get them that information."

"OK," Les interrupted, "but once you figure out all the information senders and receivers, why not connect them with a single switchboard? Don't you just end up in the same place?"

"Maybe, maybe not. But rather than starting with the idea of an intranet and then figuring out what to do with it, you should start with users, information, suppliers, and communication channels. You might find that it's not worth the trouble to crush together all internal communication."

Les was not thinking about the intranet now but about the CRM application—exactly the sort of solution looking for a problem that Allena was talking about. They had managed to select and install a complete package before asking a single question about who was supposed to get what information and how. They only had a vague idea about getting everyone everything they needed to know about customers. But where was the value?

"Aren't you just saying that you need to do a good job collecting requirements before building a system?"

"When we went to collect Web site requirements from marketing, we didn't learn anything! They were supposed to tell us what they wanted their Web site to do. But guess what? They couldn't tell us what they wanted because they didn't know."

"Maybe you were just asking the wrong questions," Les said. "When I used to do requirements gathering, we had to ask indirect questions to get useful information." Allena was impressed to hear Les anticipating her argument.

"Yep! As soon as you say 'Web site,' people start talking nonsense. If you say, 'What do you do, what is hard for you, who do you need to talk to and what about?', you get information that you can use. It's more than indirect; it's questions about their problems, not your solutions." Now it was Les' turn to be impressed.

"Way back when I used to do research and design on circuit boards, I used to tell my group 'know the problem and the solution will drop out.' Not everyone got the idea. Those who did stayed in the group." Allena tried to imagine Les as a young pioneering designer. It was not easy.

"So here's what I really think," said Allena, now in full bloom. "Let go of the assumption that your system has to deliver everything to everybody. Instead, focus on delivering something to someone. What you create doesn't have to be universally useful; it just has to deliver enough valuable information to enough people to be worth building. Find specific, important information needs and meet them."

Les dwelt on the phrase "information need." "You tell me what information you really need," he thought. "The Chief Information Officer will see that you get it." He reflected again on the CRM project. Marketing thought they needed CRM, but they couldn't say what that meant. They could only react to slick solutions and sales pitches.

"An interesting solution really motivates people, even if it is for a problem you don't have," he said.

Allena felt buoyant as she walked back to her cube. It was rare to have such a good conversation at work, and she had never had one with an executive before. What would become of this CIO? Everyone figured he would quit or be fired any day. Suppose she were in his position? Suppose the luxury of ranting about all this with no authority to change it were removed, and she suddenly had to put her philosophy into action. She felt vaguely hypocritical and small.

Alpha Design

Les stepped out of the front entrance that night and began to walk. "It all boils down to people," he thought—people who need information and people who have information. Along with all the hours he had spent studying systems, why hadn't he ever thought to study people and their information problems?

Whose job is this anyway?

Les knew the problem was that he had accepted an agenda that others had defined for him. Intranets and CRM were someone else's idea of what he should be doing. Why had he just accepted it, especially when they couldn't tell him for sure why they needed these things and left him to flounder and then (surprise) fail?

He had assumed that the new applications were like the old ones: set requirements, acquire a product, install, and implement. But in the CRM system, the Web site, and the intranet, he also needed to install an attitude in the users and implement a data model that would not stand still.

He had thought that buying the right software would be enough to acquire knowledge management. But again, it was the users and information more than the application itself that was on the critical path to success. He wondered if applications like that even belonged in his group.

"No," he thought. "As little as we know, it's still our job to make these new applications work."

In the past, he could quickly create a good data model and then not worry about getting data in. It suddenly occurred to him that now the modeling seemed to drag on and on. The structure of the data seemed to change continually; much of it was not data at all but a loose assortment of unstructured word processing and HTML files. Still, as hard as the data was to model, he realized with a start, it was also where the value lived. That's what these systems did: They delivered information. Whatever value the systems had came from that. "How do you equate business value and information delivery?" The question now seemed at the center of his entire job.

The consultant said that the digerati were his natural allies, but they thought of him as an enemy. No, as a stereotype: the bureaucratic, road-blocking, pocket-protector IT type. His first impression of the digerati came back. "I can't believe there are so many people out there doing this." The real action and innovation was outside Columbus. He had ignored and maybe permanently alienated his natural base of support.

He walked through the evening. Bits and pieces fell slowly into some loose organization. He went home and started to hammer out the details. He had two days to figure out what he would say. By about midnight, he had an outline that he would dry run with Tira. He looked forward to working with her the next day to hone the plan and reestablish some good faith.

Beta Design

Les woke up happier about work than he had been in a long time. Succeed or fail, at least he had a plan. It would surprise his team and the executives. It was still a surprise to him.

Tira was nowhere to be found that morning. When Les called her at home, she told him that she quit. She was going back to Boston and was sorry that she had been able to accomplish so little for him. She seemed perched between sad and angry.

Les was just sad. More than the board or even Garrick, he was looking forward to getting Tira behind him. The confidence he had scraped together the night before began to drain away.

He looked up to see Allena standing in his doorway.

"Want a job?" he said.

"You quitting?" she replied, picking up on what she thought was a joke then stopping short.

"What can I do for you?"

"I had a thought about what we discussed yesterday. You might be interested. I was actually over here for a meeting with Tira, but she doesn't seem to be around."

Les nodded and asked her what her idea was. It was about the debate between the two camps in IT, she said. At first, she was solidly on the user side. She always had been and she was used to fighting for it. But there was more to it. The right path was neither just erecting barriers nor just embracing the user. They did need more process, but more learning process, not administrative process. The users needed to learn how to help the IT group help them. Les' interest was kindled.

"The only problem," she concluded, "is that no one has any time. They can't find time to meet, let alone learn."

"I've noticed," Les said, "that people always have time for what they want to do. They're only too busy for what they don't want to do, or don't know how to do, or can't do."

Allena knew there was a reason she had come back to this guy's office. Les realized why he had offered her Tira's job. He decided to level with her. He moved around to the front of his desk and collapsed into the couch.

"Look," he said, "Tira just quit, and I'm inches away myself. If I don't quit today, I have to present to the board tomorrow. Then I'll probably be fired. Since yesterday I've hatched a plan to remake IT. I don't know if it even makes sense, but it's my last chance to walk out of here with my tail up."

"I was thinking about quitting too," she said, "but now I have no one to give my letter to."

"Can I help you?" she added quickly before he had to embarrass himself by asking.

"Maybe I could run my ideas by you?"

As they worked together, Les felt increasingly confident that whether any-one agreed it was the right way to go. He was back in the role of upstart and mold-breaker, and he liked it. He would say his piece and if his peers and the board didn't like it, he would find others who did. Allena was humbled again as she faced the responsibility of practicing rather than preaching. At the end of the day, neither was entirely satisfied with the plan but both were ready to try it. Whatever tomorrow would bring, today had been a great day.

A Rolling Release

Shortly before 9 AM, the boardroom was full of coffee and chatter, but Les felt like a defendant entering court. He found a seat away from the power areas of the table and looked over his notes. Was he really going to present this half-baked plan? He had an urge to leave when he felt a hand on his shoulder.

"Morning, Les," Garrick said. Registering the fear, he added, "Everything OK?"

Les did not reply.

"No plan?"

"No, I have a plan," Les returned, "I'm just not sure how it will be received."

"I knew you'd come up with something. By the way, Sandi is firing the consulting group for the same reasons she fired you. It's your move, I believe."

Les looked around the room and thought, "However little I know, they know less." By the time the meeting turned to IT, he was able to meet the eyes around the table with confidence.

"I'll begin with a report on the last year and then move on to my plan for the next year. Last year is easy. It was a failure." Sandra looked up startled and interested.

"As Sandra will confirm, I was unable to bring significant value to her division, and I alienated a large part of our staff. Most of our initiatives flopped, and you have only me to blame for it." Everyone but Garrick expected a resignation to follow.

"But don't blame me for the flops; they were inevitable. Blame me for not questioning the assignments I was given upon my arrival. Blame me for doing what I was told rather than what I should. Blame me for not knowing *what* I should do."

He had their attention now, and he felt no intimidation. It occurred to him that the perspective he was about to offer entitled him to a seat at this table.

"Any questions before I move on?" Sandra began to speak, but a look from Garrick stopped her.

"In the next year, we'll do things differently. We've always served as the place to get help implementing technology. In the future, we will only implement technology for initiatives that have specific and demonstrated business value. If we can't prove that value, we won't do the project."

Les paused here, at the weakest part of his argument.

"We have not yet entirely operationalized the concept of business value, but we have a starting place. To begin an initiative, we will require a solid justification of how the delivery of information will materially impact a business goal. We will want to know a lot about the information that is to be delivered, and about who is to receive it. Finally, we will want to know how to measure the impact of that delivery on a specific goal." He sensed that he was losing the crowd, so he put it as simply as possible.

"My group delivers information to people. Information is expensive to capture and difficult to deliver. We can't do it all, so we will only work on the information that has a proven connection to business objectives."

Wilbur raised his hand and said, "Can you tell us how you will measure the importance of information in order to prioritize your projects?" Yes, that was the hard part.

"You will tell me," Les said. "For example, what do you want this company to do?"

"A lot of things. Chief among them is to expand while maintaining our focus on customer service."

"Do you think that delivering information to people has anything to do with that goal?"

"Of course. As I've said many times, we need to get the experience out of the heads of our older staff and into the heads of the newcomers."

"My team can't help you reach into people's heads and pull out experience. We can gather words, sounds, and pictures, and move them from one computer to another. So, can you be more specific about the information we can help you deliver?"

"You helped me deliver my own words," Wilbur said. "How about delivering information about who the experienced people are and helping them share their ideas?"

At first, Les thought Wilbur was jesting. Then he realized that Wilbur probably never even looked at Knowledge Central.

"Yes," he returned, "we tried something like that. Few people cared enough to give us any of that information, and we couldn't make them do it. We ended up spending a lot of money to look foolish. In the future, we will be sure that we can fill whatever systems we build.

"So, given your desire that we expand while maintaining our marketing position, are these two types of information the most important kinds to invest in?"

Wilbur shrugged. "I don't know if they are the most important, but they are important."

"There are a lot of important types of information," Les said. "It is my responsibility to make sure that we spend your money on only the most important of them. I will work with you, our staff, and our users to decide what information, and, in turn, what systems are worth investing in.

"In the case of the expansion, it turns out, that our 'young Turks' have suggested other kinds of information that that they feel are very important."

Les handed out a sheet of paper titled *Ideas from the Field that Support the Expansion*. He and Allena had distilled it from the consultant's report.

"Which of these ideas is the best? We all have opinions, but in the future, we will have a set of specific criteria for determining the information that has the best chance of returning value."

"And you feel that you can come up with and evenly apply these criteria?" Garrick prompted.

Les could have just said yes. Instead, he said, "That is clearly the hardest but most important thing. We need to base our IT investment strategy on a tenable model of information value. Frankly, IT should not decide what information is most important, but we need this information to do our jobs. So I am willing to get the ball rolling."

"So, what does this all mean for the Web site?" Sandra asked. Les tried hard to speak without overtones.

"There is no such thing as the Web site," he returned.

Sandra snorted.

"I'm not being facetious. We thought at first that there was a single Web site that we could launch and revise. We found out the hard way," now looking at Garrick, "that a lot of people use the Web for a lot of jobs. We don't have a site, so much as a communication channel."

"I know I have a Web site," Sandra said. "I see it on the bills every month." There was a brief chuckle and a shuffling of bodies around the table.

"Yes, you do, but we don't. The Web is a way of communicating, it's not a single site. People across AFS use it for a lot of different reasons. It's not marketing's vehicle, or anybody else's vehicle, any more than the telephone or email is."

"Your responsibility, Sandi," he said, surprising himself with the use of that name, "is to use the Web and all other channels to do the work of marketing. My responsibility is to make sure that you and everyone else can use those channels as effectively as possible. That's why I say there is no such thing as *the* Web site. There are lots of Web sites; yours is just the most expensive." The chuckles grew louder now, and Les managed to crack a smile.

The room was with Les now. Sandra knew better than to oppose. But Les would need to have more than smoke and mirrors the next time they met.

"There is also no such thing as the intranet. Despite our efforts to jam all internal Web sites into one big site, they just don't fit." The crowd was getting lost again, and his time was almost up, so Les decided to make his last point.

"My group is here to enable the strategic use of information in AFS. Part of that means helping to define what is and is not strategic. The other part is building our communication technology so that people who should be using it can be using it. We are not here to build *the* intranet; we are here to give you the ability to use intranets and whatever else you need to deliver the information that helps you hit your targets.

"Here is what I need from you: Stop talking to me about the intranet, knowledge management, and the Web site. Start talking to me about who needs to get what information in order that you get something that you want."

Les sat down to a silent room.

"Thanks for that, Les," said Garrick "The half I understood sounded good. I'm sure we will be seeing some detailed plans around your new approach very soon. Are there any questions for Les?" There were no questions.

Les tried to judge the reaction, but they had moved on. Was that too vague? Is that what Garrick had meant? Was he too blunt with Wilbur? Was this all just a bunch of hot air with no teeth behind it? He knew from other board meetings that no reaction, especially from Wilbur, was a good reaction. He figured that he had gotten his foot in the door just before it slammed on him. But it was just a foot. He would have to pry that door wide open before his future here, or anywhere else, as the Chief of Information was assured.

Part 2

Get Perspective

Information is funny. It is the simplest, most natural thing. We create and consume it all day long. Yet when we try to discuss it, we realize at once just how little we know about it and how far we are from any sort of agreement on what information is or how we should work with it in our organizations. To some, information is a witch's brew concocted by the practitioner of the persuasive arts to magically convince anyone of anything. To others, information is no more than data to be stored, retrieved, and rendered.

Your organization might be a bit confused about information.
Figure out why you should care, and then teach everyone else.

In fact, information exists simultaneously at both these extremes (and a few more as well). You have to understand and harness the persuasive impact of information and practice its arcane arts. But you also have to manage it as an enterprise resource in databases and Web pages. In this section, I'll lay out a simple definition of information that will help you avoid the conceptual traps people often fall into. I'll also lay out fundamental arguments that you can use to clearly and simply state the value of information.

Chapters in This Part

Chapter 5: Know What Information Is – Information is communication. Information systems simply help you talk to people who are not in front of you. Information is all the common forms of recorded communication we are interested in consuming. Our need to transact business through communication has not changed, but it has broadened tremendously.

Chapter 6: Know Why Information Matters – All organizations want people to believe, know, or do things, so all organizations need to effectively use information. Information persuades; that is how it can work on behalf of your organization. It is just as important to understand and use this aspect of information as it is to build systems. Our old ideas about data are still important, but they need to be accompanied by new ideas about information.

Know What Information Is

Information is communication. Information systems simply help you talk to people who are not in front of you. Information is all the common forms of recorded communication we are interested in consuming. Our need to transact business through communication has not changed, but it has broadened tremendously.

If you strip away all of the technology and terminology we use to describe information systems, what do you have left? A simple and utterly commonplace idea: Information systems help you talk to people who are not in front of you.

Cut through the morass of confusion and take a simple but effective attitude toward information.

Computer-based systems, as well as the systems that preceded them (print, sound, and moving images), have all served the same purpose. Those who know would like to speak to those who do not know. Time and space do not permit them to do so in person, so they send their words and images through some proxy. Whether the proxy is a town crier, a Web site, or a wiki, the result is the same. We organize and present ourselves to the people we want to speak to using some intermediary source. Technology has battered back time and space until, for the first time in history, with enough money, you can talk to anyone, anywhere, anytime. But don't be disoriented by this extraordinary circumstance. The fundamental parts of the story remain. What we want to say has not changed.

Information Is Simple but Subtle

Debates rage on about what is and is not information. Engineers and physicists talk about nonrandom fluctuations being information. Biologists talk about stimuli and nerve impulses being information to the brain. Journalists talk about stories, and logicians talk about facts. People who call themselves information scientists argue without end about the nature of information and what should be included in its definition. I've almost given up on these debates, feeling like it might be better to use different words rather than trying to pin such a vague one down.

Yet, it is the natural term to use for the subject matter we are discussing. I've often used the word "content" as a sort of stand-in for information, but except in specific circles, the word "content" does more to obscure than clarify my meaning. I want to use the word "information," but to avoid the tiresome debate, I want to stick to a very common sense definition.

Information is all the common forms of recorded communication we are interested in consuming, including:

- Text, such as articles, books, and news

- Sound, such as music, recorded conversations, and readings

- Images, such as photos and illustrations

- Motion, such as video and animations

- Computer files, such as spreadsheets, slide shows, databases, and other proprietary files

This definition of information gives us a clear and simple starting place for understanding information management.

Information management is collecting and delivering the sorts of recorded communications that we all want to consume. You manage information because you think that organizing your collection and distribution will return more than it costs. Conversely, if you don't believe that the cost of organizing all this information will pay off, then there is no reason to manage your information. I can't stress this point enough. I'll come back to it over and over again in this book.

The big problem with using the word "information" is that a lot of people already have a claim on it. There are innumerable information systems that do not have a single item of what I would call information in them. There are Information Technology (IT) groups that avoid my kind of information completely.

 Should we continue to create print publications?

 It's not about print vs. online. It's about important vs. unimportant publications. Any publication should be judged on the same basis: how important it is to getting us to our goals. More specifically, tell me what information the publication delivers to which people, and I will give you some indication of how important it is relative to the other ones we create.

I have decided to use the term "information" anyway. In doing so, I have thrown my lot in with all those others who assert a claim on the term. I have no illusions that my meaning and use of the term "information" will prevail. I just feel that it's time to come out of the closet and confess that what I am interested in is not some specialized thing called content but the bigger thing called information.

When I talk about information management systems, I am not talking about other sorts of computer systems, such as manufacturing applications, financial automation, scientific systems, desktop software and server systems. These are all important, and they all use the word information to describe what they process, but they are not the subject of this book.

The subject of this book is the kinds of systems that gather and distribute the text, pictures, sound, and motion that we humans are most interested in consuming. This kind of information, which everyone wants all the time, is also the kind of information that we have so far not been very good at delivering.

Electronic Information Is Still Information

It's sad but true that humans have not had much new to say since the first language was invented. From a business standpoint, what this boils down to is that if you understood your customers (or members, citizens, constituents, etc.) before electronic publication and knew how to talk to them then, the new technology just gives you more ways to have those same conversations. If you didn't know how to talk to all these people before, no amount of new technology will talk to them for you. The new technology may, however, force you to confront your communication difficulties instead of ignoring them as you could in the past.

Although electronic information does not change the nature of information, it does bring a quantitative change in our ability to use it. Specifically, electronic information delivery increases:

- **Ubiquity** – Parts of your information base can appear on any computer screen anywhere there is connectivity. Time and space are no longer barriers to communication.

- **Depth** – You can deliver as much detail and background as you can manage to create in a convenient and easy-to-consume fashion. Rather than racks full of catalogs and technical documentation, a simple URL is all that is needed to fully detail your organization's offerings.

- **Speed** – The slowness of your human processes is the only necessary delay between the creation of information and its general availability. Second-by-second changes to information are now possible and entirely practical.

- **Personalization** – Technology now allows you to tailor information precisely based on a user profile. Your ability to do so is only limited by understanding your audiences and your ability to collect profile data.

- **Interaction** – Many of the newer channels (the Web, mobile phones, etc.) allow easy two-way communication. You can now intermingle information and computer functionality, and your audiences can now immediately talk back.

In short, fast, deep, and sophisticated communication is now available all the time. Nothing else about information has changed.

eBusiness Is Still Business

Electronic information is the foundation of eBusiness, which means delivering any part of your business information, or functionality, to any audience anytime, anywhere. But just as electronic information is just information, eBusiness is just business and the dictates of business remain the same:

- **Know your audiences** – To know your audiences, you must study them to understand what they want and how they want it. You then segment them into groups based on traits you can discover and track. Finally, for each audience, you create a value proposition, including what the audience wants, what you want from them, and how you are going to give value equal to what you want from them.

- **Know your business** – To know your business, you first must study it to understand how it can be segmented into small, useful information and functionality parts. You must name and organize the parts, and understand how the parts are created, maintained, delivered, and destroyed.

- **Relate the business to the audience** – You need to decide which audience wants what information and functionality in which contexts (on which pages, on which sites, in what other publications, and so on). You must then create a set of rules so that staff can easily direct the right information into the right delivery channel.

Organizations have been doing this more or less formally forever, but we are still working out how to digitize and automate this process. Clearly, however, you can use information management to help do eBusiness. That is, you can create a process to collect, manage, and publish information to a set of target audiences in order to forward your business aims.

Know Why
Information Matters

All organizations want people to believe, know, or do things,
so all organizations need to effectively use information.
Information persuades; that is how it can work on behalf of
your organization. It is just as important to understand and use
this aspect of information as it is to build systems. Our old ideas
about data are still important, but they need to be accompanied
by new ideas about information.

Most organizations say information matters but behave as if it did not. In the large majority of organizations that I have worked with, information is treated as a necessary evil on the road to more significant activities. If organizations could reduce the cost of creating information to zero, they would. If they

There's no need to squabble over who is bigger. Both information and technology matter, and each one deserves a separate and equal focus in your IT group.

could get away with producing no information at all, they would. They have no unified notion of what kind of information they should be producing and no guidelines or policies for what constitutes high quality. Every information producer is left to his or her own wits to figure out what information to produce, how to make it good, and to whom it should be distributed. The production of information rarely appears in anyone's job description or performance review. In short, information is not important.

On the other hand, I've never met anyone who would dispute that information is critical to his or her organization's success. Everyone agrees that we are in the Information Age and that information is an "asset." But these often amount to empty platitudes; they contain no actionable statements to make them real. So, does information matter or not? It does!

Information is a powerful motivator. Well designed and wisely delivered, it will pull people toward what you want them to know, believe, or do. There is nothing Machiavellian about this; it is just a fact of our existence and not an especially strange or mysterious one. When we consume information, it becomes part of what we know or believe. When we act, we act based on what we know or believe. Everyone knows about the evils of manipulation by information, but the vast majority of information we produce is not intended to control or unfairly influence. It informs, and its purposes are as varied and diverse as the organizations that create and deliver it.

All organizations want people to believe, know, or do things. So all organizations need to effectively use information. For some organizations, however, the need goes further. Information is their product. Many commercial organizations sell information. Governments output information such as laws, regulations, and policy statements. Libraries supply information to patrons. Nonprofit organizations issue reports and recommendations. All of these organizations produce information like a baker produces bread.

If your organization wants something from people, you will have to attend to information. If information is your product, you will have even more reason to pay attention. As simple as it is to say, it can be really hard to do. Which information should you give to which people so that they might have which particular thoughts or perform which specific actions? How do you get a hold of this information and how do you get it to people in such a way that they can and will consume it? It is relatively easy to judge the quality of a piece of bread, but how can you judge the quality of an item of information?

The answer to these questions is also easy to state but hard to do. To make effective use of information, you have to craft a value proposition for each kind of important person you interact with:

We will provide you with the information that you really want, and, in return, you will give back some of the value to us.

For example, this book contains information that is delivered to you by me. Here is my value proposition to you:

If you will buy this book, I will provide you with valuable ideas on how to use information to get your organization what it wants. I'll help you by sharing what I have figured out about information management. I would like all of you to help me by believing that I am a smart guy and showering me with fame. I would like a very small fraction of you to hire me and shower me with fortune.

I hope that I have understood you well enough to provide the right information for you. I hope that if you consume my information, you will be able to find the answers to the questions I have proposed or to direct others to do so. I hope that, having found answers, you will be able and willing to direct your staff to turn answers into systems that bring tangible and specific benefits to your organization. I hope that if I do all that for you, you will do something for me as well.

Ultimately, information matters because it is how we interact with other people. More practically, information matters because it can have a material impact on whatever goals you pursue. If you can somehow manage to get ahead of the flood of information and harness some of its persuasive force, you can become an indispensable asset to your organization.

Information Persuades

Persuasion means getting someone to know or do something. Rhetoric is the study of how to use information to persuade. If you want to use information to get people to help your organization, you might want to look further into this subject. Rhetoric is not only for information that is meant to spur very specific actions (like voting for a candidate or buying toothpaste). It is for all information. Even the plainest product data sheet has a persuasive purpose. It gets the reader to know something new. If it didn't, why would you bother to create it? Even if your goal is simply to inform your audiences rather than convince them to buy something, the resources you put into information collection and dissemination will always have to be justified based on some value they will return to you. Thus, there is always a reason to think more deeply about how information persuades.

From poets to politicians and from filmmakers to direct marketers, virtually all disciplines use information as a persuasive tool. We are used to thinking of authors that have some sort of "gift for communication" as the source of information. But there are any number of other sources of information talent. Of course, marketing and public relations departments are full of communication graduates who know and apply rhetoric. And anyone who is good at media (producing photos, illustrations, and audio or video segments) has to be skilled at drawing the eye or ear and making a case. Cartoonists seem to have a particularly sharp sense of rhetoric. All of these people craft a message that is meant to move an audience toward some notion or action.

Covering rhetoric in detail and discussing its impact on information management is worth a book of its own. Here, I would simply like to point out a few of its commonsense high points.

- **Arguments** – The central concept of rhetoric is the argument. Arguments persuade. There are many taxonomies of argument methods and types, but they all share the common thrust that you need to tailor your arguments to the audience receiving them and the claims that the information itself can support.

- **Credibility** – The person who is making an argument matters a lot. Again, there are plenty of theories and advice about how to be believable, but they all start with the careful consideration of the attitudes and dispositions of your audience.

- **Context** – It matters what information a person has previously consumed and what his or her prior experiences are when confronting your information. It also matters what surrounds the information in your publications and what information is next to what other information.

- **Narrative** – The story is the most basic form of communication. Why go with the idea that "business information" is just the facts when we all know that a good story—one with characters we care about, doing important things—is a powerful memory aid and an even more powerful motivator?

- **Style** – How you say something can be just as important as what you say. Are you speaking to a respected peer? A newbie? An old-timer? If you make the wrong guess, you may communicate only your incompetence. If you believe that you can avoid guessing by using completely neutral language, you may not communicate at all.

You can use these and other rhetorical considerations to make every Web page or other act of communication as effective as possible. The problem, of course, is that you don't have the time or resources for carefully tailoring each Web page. Instead, you have to come up with a rhetorical approach that can be applied automatically across audiences, information, and publications. In an information management system, you will have to gather and tag your information in such a way that it can deliver the right arguments in the right way to a variety of audiences on a variety of platforms.

This is clearly not an easy task and one you might like to avoid. But if you want to avoid these issues altogether, there is one last lesson from rhetoric that I would like to share. No decision on argument, credibility, context, and the rest is still a decision. Your audience will make theses discriminations whether you want them to or not. They will find and evaluate the arguments, judge your credibility, and so on. They can't help doing so because it is an integral part of understanding. To have some measure of control over the impact your information has, you have to recognize and master the rhetoric of your information to whatever extent you can.

People within or outside your organization who are members of an important audience can help you identify "the available means of persuasion." People who are deeply immersed in the information you want to deliver can help too. Once identified, the rhetorical approach has to be tied to a user profile on one hand and a content model on the other. The user profile states what kinds of people your approach targets. The content model states exactly what attributes or elements of the information have been refined to make an impact on those people. It is a long way from the realization that rhetoric is important to having it as an active part of your information systems. On the other hand, if you simply pass on whatever you get from contributors to your audiences, you may get the facts but miss the argument and persuasion that those facts can support.

Match the "I" and the "T"

There are a lot of things that an IT (Information Technology) group might do, but for the purposes of this book, the point of the IT department is to deliver information. If everyone is getting all the information they need to get to make your organization successful, then the IT group is doing its job. If people are not getting what they need, IT has more work to do. If IT can get all the "I" to everyone using only a little "T," that's fine. If IT has a lot of good "T" but little "I" is reaching its intended audience, that's not fine.

Think hard about this. If you won't give this proposition a chance, you might as well not continue on. But this pernicious little thought might just change forever what you think you are here to do. You will be forced into the proposition, for example, that part of your job is to get people to talk to each other. You will have to embrace rather than flee from the never-ending process of defining the words we use. You will need to make peace with word processing files and other unwieldy forms of "unstructured information." If you put information on par with technology, you might be led in a number of uncomfortable directions, and these are precisely the directions you will need to get information to work for your organization.

Most IT groups define themselves as "the technology guys." If it has to do with computers and making them work, they are the ones to see. More specifically, they claim the following organizational territory:

- Creating and establishing strategy and policy concerning the technology that the organization should use and how it should be used for business benefit

- Procuring and maintaining computer hardware, including the wires and switches that connect them within and outside the organization

- Procuring and maintaining Commercial Off-The-Shelf (COTS) software (any software product that the organization buys and deploys widely in the organization)

- Supporting the hardware and software the organization owns

These are the basic functions of a modern IT organization. Together they constitute a maintenance function. Just as other groups maintain the physical facilities, the IT group maintains the computer (and increasingly the telecommunications) facilities. While important, these functions are not what we are here to discuss.

Many IT groups add a development function to the technology maintenance functions. Development functions include:

- Creating and establishing strategy and policy on how software development should be used by the organization for business benefit

- Performing business analysis and requirements gathering for business computer systems

- Developing or customizing business computer systems

- Overseeing deployment, training, maintenance, and the continuing evolution of business computer systems

Together, the infrastructure and development functions cover the "T" in IT. All the "T" functions are important, but what we are here to discuss is the "I" in IT.

The term Information Technology, or Information and Communication Technology (ICT), implies that the group's focus is on the kind of technology that delivers information. I (and many others) prefer to think of this group as information *and* technology. To remain at the forefront of the organization, the IT group needs to embrace the "I" in its name and augment its existing technology functions with an information function, including:

- Creation and establishment of strategy and policy on the proper use of information by the organization for business benefit

- Information and process analysis for business information systems

- Design and development or procurement of facilities and software to implement the information policy

- Deployment, training, maintenance, and continuing evolution of the information in information systems

If you believe, as many IT leaders do, that a) information policy is someone else's business, b) information analysis is just a part of requirements gathering, and c) information systems are *just* business computer systems, then the information function effectively dissolves (as it does in many organizations) into the software development function.

If you believe, as I do, that information is different, then it deserves a separate and equal focus in your organization to be done well. Information strategy is different, information analysis is different, information implementation is different, and information maintenance and support is different. Information systems require information teams and information skills.

I did software development for a number of years before information made it to the screen. In the late 1980s, when the ability to display formatted text and pictures (and later sound and video) came along, I realized just how different information is from the rest of software development. All of a sudden my teams were filled with writers and editors, graphic artists, and designers, sound engineers, and videographers. Their concerns were worlds away from—but just as valid as—those of the programmers and architects I was used to. Audience, tone, context, format, and presentation were juxtaposed and vying for attention with users, code, modules, algorithms, and executables. On the one side were the people who specialized in information; on the other were the people who did technology. When this arrangement worked well, it did so because there was an equal partnership between worlds. When it failed, it was because the techies held the power and were not willing to share.

Many people, within IT and outside it, say that this is too big of a change. IT departments are too "in to" technology to ever give information a proper place. IT professionals avoid anything that feels like the English, business, or theater arts department. Many business- or information-oriented managers believe that their IT group is incapable of doing "real" information management. Some organizations have created "new media" groups that bypass this perceived IT blind spot. But information and technology are so intertwined today that it is far easier to stretch IT to meet these new challenges than to build a parallel new department. This option increases IT's ability to do more and different projects. More importantly, a stronger information focus can add relevance to the advice that comes out of IT. It can deepen and diversify the services that IT provides.

The other option, which many organizations have taken, is to create a separate information management (IM) group. (I'm not sure why after doing this more organizations don't strip the IT group of its "I.") If the separate IM group prioritizes information and does not end up yet another IT group, it can do a lot to advance the cause of information. Still, the more the IM group succeeds in managing information, the more closely it will become tied to information technology. So other than politics, why bother to split?

However you end up lumping and splitting in order to do information management well, you need a solid and equal partnership between the engineering attitude of traditional techies and the humanistic focus of the new media types.

Sort Out Information from Data

Computers were built to process data. Data consists of small snippets of computer information that are mostly numbers and short phrases. We invented databases (bases of data) to organize and hold vast quantities of these little snippets.

But beginning in the 1990s, we decided that we wanted computers to deal with more than just data. We wanted them to deliver information rich in context and meaning. We wanted computers to do more than finely grind through mountains of data snippets. Today, we want computers to sift through mountains of large, complete chunks of information and deliver the ones we want most at the moment. We also want computers to deliver information of the quality we have come to expect from books, magazines, radio, TV, and film.

Although users' needs and expectations have changed, the guts of the computer have not. Ten years ago, most people came to computers to input, process, and output data. Today, most people come to find and consume information. Unfortunately, at the base of all computer technology remains the assumption that you can reduce any problem to input, processing, and output. Computers work best with a set of simple instructions and mounds of data.

From the computer programmer's perspective, there is no such thing as information; it's all data. Any information inside a computer is rightly called data, but that misses the point. Data is the stuff that scientists, engineers, and finance staff deal with daily. The rest of us want information. In fact, from the user's perspective, there is no such thing as data. Users expect everything they get from a computer to be rich, context-laden information,

Is it even possible to use computers and their data technologies to manage and deliver very nondata-like information? Yes, but it will be far easier to do when someday someone invents a computer that recognizes the true complexity of information and the problems we use information to solve. At that point, being a computer scientist will begin to feel a lot like being a writer or artist, and we won't have all these disputes between the "T" and "I" in our organizations.

The trick to information management, in an age when the technology is still data-driven, is to effectively use the data technologies to store and deliver but not to understand information. Today's computers have massive information storage capacity. They can automate the delivery of information across a variety of platforms. But they have no ability to automate the understanding of information. However, if you take the time to understand your information, you can augment the information with data (metadata) that a computer can use to store, retrieve, and deliver it. If your consumers can figure out how your metadata relates to the information they are looking for, they will be able to use the metadata to find the information using a dumb computer.

Even if you really understand the information, you may not have the time and resources needed to add the data to it. And your consumers may not even understand the information, let alone the metadata. Still, the gains you can make from understanding and metatagging your information can be worth the cost. To make matters even worse, there is no magic dividing line between data and information. In fact, it has become critically important that data and information sit side by side on many Web pages and other information outlets.

Data, of course, remains important. I'm sure there are plenty of very critical data-only applications running in your organization. But information is important too, and it's getting more important as computers are becoming the source of information for more and more people.

So you can try to remain back in the old world of data technologies and data management but it won't work. You can attempt to ignore information and the more modern techniques of information management, but in the long run, it will spell your demise. You may want simple solutions, data that behaves and an algorithmic approach to all problems, but the world around you now demands complex systems that process misbehaving information and coax context and intelligence out of their essentially unintelligent computer programs. So, there is the problem: Old attitudes and old methods clash with new needs. But what's the solution? Read on.

Part 3

Lead Up

Your teams probably do not expect you to lead information if you have not been leading it so far. Your bosses, on the other hand, surely expect you to lead it. They expect you to be the person who knows what to do with the organization's information. However, your bosses are not likely to be any more enlightened about information than your teams. They likely hold that information is important, that the organization is not doing all it could with information, and that IT is costing a lot and not always repaying the cost. Other than these vague concepts, it is unlikely that the people above you in the organization can tell you what to do. You will probably have to figure it out yourself and get your peers and bosses to agree.

Don't hesitate. Create a place for yourself at the leadership table
with information, determination, patience, and chutzpah.

This situation is not for the weak of mind or spirit. It is really tough to have to invent your job and sell it to people who are nowhere near understanding what you are talking about. Other executives may be good or bad, right or wrong, but what they are supposed to do and how they are supposed to do it is well established. Even if you know nothing about operations, it is fairly clear what a COO (Chief Operating Officer) does and how she does it. CIOs, on the other hand, often have undefined or at least under-defined responsibilities. This, of course, is a great opportunity for you to create your own job. You can define what it means to be in charge of information in your organization—if you have the wits, determination, patience, and guts to put it all together.

Chapters in This Part:

Chapter 7: Own Information – Be prepared to use information to solve problems. Convince everyone from the board on down that information can solve problems and add to the "bottom line." Develop your ability to see every problem from the perspective of information. Chart and articulate a long-term vision for what information could be doing for you.

Chapter 8: Know the Goals – If you don't know the goals of your organization, you can only progress against them by chance. If you do not know which goals are best served by information, then you cannot design information systems that forward them. If you can't measure progress against your goals, then you can't know if you have served them.

Chapter 9: Create an Enterprise Strategy – As the leader of information, you must be able and willing to form simple propositions about what information should do for your organization. You must also be willing to reiterate your propositions over and over again. At some point, every conversation needs to come back to one of your propositions about what information could be doing for the organization. Use the idea of Strategy Statements to develop simple, repeatable statements about what information management you should do.

Chapter 10: Devolve Ownership – Once you have firmly established your ownership of information management, act quickly to spread that ownership to the rest of the organization. Continue to lead the enterprise, but shift strategy creation and updates to the business units and move ownership of audiences and information to the people who know them best.

Chapter 7

Own Information

*Be prepared to use information to solve problems.
Convince everyone from the board on down that information
can solve problems and add to the "bottom line." Develop
your ability to see every problem from the perspective of
information. Chart and articulate a long-term vision for
what information could be doing for you.*

So what would it mean to be an executive in charge of information and who
is relevant to your CEO and board? In essence, it means that you are always
ready to show how the appropriate distribution of information can help
achieve an objective. If the Marketing Officer says, "We need to expand to a
national presence," you would be able to immediately suggest ways that existing and new information sources and systems can help make that happen.

Chart a confident course through the waters of information
management for your unsure and sometime reluctant colleagues.

With a small amount of effort from you and your staff, you should be able
to present a cogent plan for how information could support the initiative or

better, how information could drive the initiative. When the CEO blithely says, "We need an intranet," you would be in a position to ask why and to lead the CEO to either sharpen her idea or happily abandon it.

Today's CIOs often hide behind technology. They talk bits and bytes when they could provide simple answers in plain language to questions that really matter. They focus on procurement, development, and infrastructure and avoid the more important questions of how information can advantage the organization.

The Light Is Better Over Here

I am reminded at least once a day of this joke/parable that seems to apply to so many situations in and around information management.

My friend lost his wallet on the north side of the street. It was already night when I came across him, and he was looking carefully for his wallet—but he was on the south side of the street.

"Why are you looking over here?" I asked. "Didn't you lose your wallet on the other side?"

"I did," he replied. "But the light is better over here."

We all prefer to search where the light is better. The light over technology is bright enough to provoke lots of important discussion. It is not hard to make an entire department out of these discussions. The light over information is dim. But as the joke makes painfully clear, no amount of searching through the territory of technology will help you find the answer to what to do with your information.

Whatever you want to do with technology or information, it will undoubtedly be costly and time-consuming. So it had better be important! Executives know this from experience: Technology always costs a lot but does not always accomplish a lot. Without an information leader to plot a reasonable and rational way to manage technology expenditures, what options do executives have when considering information systems? They can do the following:

- Question all technology expenditures because they don't know how to control their costs.

- Insist upon a return on investment (ROI) as the sole justification for an information management system. As I explain further in the section "Nonstrategic Projects" in Chapter 16, Lead Information Projects, not all information management systems do or should save money.

- Let technology cost what it needs to without serious oversight or constraint (the 1990s approach).

The person in charge of information could provide an alternative vision of driving technology expenditures for the greatest return against established goals. It is likely that no one else has figured out the relationship between value and information. Few have probably even thought to try, and those who did try failed. The person in charge of information, however, is clearly the one to work on the problem.

Of course, you don't have to figure it all out by yourself. You have a staff and peers to help you. But this is not something to be lightly delegated. The less you know about the best uses of information in your organization, the less relevant you will be to your teams as well to your bosses. If you don't have time to figure out information, who should? If other concerns are more important than understanding and taking charge of your organization's information, then maybe someone else should lead. If you don't think the task is interesting or useful, or if you can't make it happen, then definitely someone else should lead.

Take Charge

If you do not already have authority to own information management in your organization, just go ahead and appoint yourself the interim king. This move is not as strange as it might seem. I've seen it happen throughout my career. The one who takes charge is in charge, especially when the person takes charge of something that no one else in the organization even knows exists!

Your reign as monarch, however, should be short. As soon as possible, you should impanel an information governance body and give it a charter and rules of order. If and when the governors truly take charge, you can retire to your IT ranch and just do projects. If, as is much more likely, the legislature never does become ready, you can continue to preside over them and keep them productive.

One way or another, you need to take charge of information to do your job. Without a solid foundation of rules and rule making and enforcement procedures, your group will fail. If no one else will take control to get information and its management organized, why not you?

Just because you need to own information, however, doesn't mean you deserve to own it. What do you alone bring to the table? What talents and perspective can you tap or develop that put you at the head of information management? How about the following for a start:

- You clearly articulate and always push for the "big picture" of how information serves goals and how systems serve information. You are able to say what information management is and why it is a central part of your group and your organization.

- You can make quick decisions that you can justify with compelling arguments. This decisiveness plays well outside your group and within it. Outside, you can lead others to recognize how information can (or cannot) impact their objectives. Within your group, you know which projects to begin, which to end, and what to do at critical junctures within a project.

- You can arbitrate between competing views and have the authority to make your arbitration stick. Authority comes from many places, but the kind of authority that is most pertinent here is derived from a well-considered, proven set of judgment criteria. These criteria help you determine which ideas, systems, or other proposals are worthy and which are not.

Ultimately, you can lead because you always know what to do. For example, as leader of information, you should always be:

- **Pushing a vision** – When someone looks at you, the first thing that comes to mind is your vision for the IT group. You have given your spiel so many times that it is impossible to forget it. You have said it in so many ways that it is impossible not to understand it.

- **Pushing a strategy** – Using my ideas or, even better, your own, you have grasped the exact steps needed to turn your vision into reality.

- **Promoting** – You are confident in yourself and in your team's abilities. You are ready and willing to promote your team to the rest of the organization. You are prepared to overcome whatever old baggage your team carries and then to educate, persuade, and outmaneuver groups that don't believe in you.

- **Forming plans** – You have a 5- to 10-year-plan even though you know the technology will turn over two or three times in that period. Your plan is based on your goals, audiences, and information, which do not turn over as quickly (see the section titled "Make Strategy Statements" in Chapter 9, Create an Enterprise Strategy).

- **Prioritizing** – You can articulate specific parameters for determining what makes one project more important than another.

- **Evaluating** – You can accurately establish the contribution of each project your group executes. You know exactly how projects fit together to realize the wider strategy.

- **Questioning** – You ask hard questions. You ask your teams to justify their actions and you are willing to shut down projects that cannot justify themselves. You challenge your peers and bosses when they make unjustified claims about systems or new technologies.

The real job of a leader is not to know *how*, but to know *what* (not how to do the work, but what work needs to be done). If project sponsors are confused about what information can and should do for them, they will give your team inadequate and conflicting instructions about what work to do. As the beacon of "what-ness," you should be able to cut through the fog of these confused sponsors and drifting teams and always know what to do next.

Your immediate needs as a leader of systems can push you naturally to became the leader of information. No one will question why you need to know about information to build systems. However, there is no easy road to a comprehensive strategy that is immediately actionable by your team but provides guidance for the long term. If you don't have them, get the skills you need to drive that road.

Perform for the Board

In most organizations, the board is the highest governing body. Even within single sectors, boards operate differently. Across sectors, the contrasts are more pronounced. But in any organization, the board looks after the longest term health and goals of the organization, including its choice of leaders.

You deserve to be in front of the board if you can prove that information not only advances goals but is central to meeting goals. Clearly, this should be the case if you create information as a product, in the same way that the assembly line is central to meeting goals in an automotive corporation. But the board does not care about the assembly line per se; it cares about radical improvements to the assembly line that confer significant advantages to the organization. Similarly, the board should not care about the particular systems that the IT group creates, but how information can confer significant advantage to the organization.

Why should you be on the executive team?

 I can directly help this organization reach its goals. My group's expertise is one of your most powerful tools for getting what you want.

If you believe and can clearly articulate how information is central to the progress of your organization, then you belong in front of the board. If you can prove that information is the primary key to understanding the organization and to driving it forward overall, maybe the board needs to appoint you to lead the whole organization. This is not as unlikely as it may appear. Why are so many CEOs from finance? Because they believed and could convincingly demonstrate that money-colored glasses were the best ones to wear to understand and drive the organization forward.

 What value does your group bring to this organization?

 Does information bring value to this organization? If so, then we do too. No one else understands as we do how to squeeze value out of information. No one else has a practical method for deciding which information to invest in. No one else has the tools, staff, and procedures to make sure that valuable information can make it from creation to consumption. But our biggest value comes not when we do all this ourselves, but rather, when we teach the rest of you how to do it as well. Of course, we are still learning, but we are and will remain ahead of the rest of the organization and ready to move us all forward.

I don't want to give the impression that you need to be a star to appear before the board. It makes a lot sense for you to present current initiatives, progress against goals, and contribution to the key indicators of success on an ongoing basis just as any other executive would. If you simply demonstrate that information concerns are relevant to discussions at the board level, you will be ahead of most organizations. But if you develop a strategy along the lines of what I outline, you should have more than just the standard stuff to bring to the board.

Make Long-Term Plans

Technology is constantly changing, the needs of the organization are changing, system requirements change, and even the definition of "system" evolves as we come more and more into the computer age. Does it make sense then to plan more than six months or a year out? Yes, if your plans are not for adopting technology but for delivering information to people. Technology can change on the timescale of months. Your goals, audiences, and information evolve over years. Unlike technology, they are not swept away by the latest great idea.

 Do we need to staff up?

 How will the people we need to hire continue to help us over the next five years? Let me show you my long-term plans. Let me know how these people would fit in. Also, what are you doing now to make sure that the staff we have today will continue to grow to meet this plan?

Your information strategy defines the distant horizon of satisfied information needs that you are heading toward. Your plans chart the best path to that horizon. Of course, the horizon recedes as you approach it, and you need to modify your course as you go along, but these things all happen gradually. There is no reason to stop planning because of them.

The continual throughput of technology is actually an excellent reason to plan. Without the rudder of a long-term plan, your team will be tossed about by the shifting waves of the "next big thing." Against the background of ever-changing technology, you need a stable yardstick with which to measure progress toward authentic, articulated goals. And if you ever expect to get leverage across projects or allow your limited staff do the limitless work of providing information, you had better have some sort of a plan that transcends the timeframe of any technologies you currently use.

You also have to train your organization to come to you with unmet information needs rather than the name of some new technology that they "just have to adopt." You can do this training only if you yourself are sure of what an information need is and how your team can meet it better over time regardless of technology (or perhaps in spite of it).

As usual, you have to begin with a strategy. Without that fixed point on the horizon, you can forget about navigating even to the next quarter. But with a good strategy, you are in a position to put together long-term plans including:

- You can plan projects that deliver a particular kind of information to a particular audience. Initial projects for an audience identify their information needs. Future projects can serve them more and more. You can use one project to develop a particular information type that you know you will use later in other projects. The sequencing of projects can span many years. You can figure out the technology base for the future projects later. The plan does not chart the platform. It tells you when the project needs to begin delivering information to give you the desired gains against goals at the time you need them.

- You can plan incrementally and progressively to build bases of shared information or delivery channels (internal Web sites, handheld devices, printed alerts, and so on). Each iteration of the info-base or channel serves some specific goal. Over the longer term, however, the goals can get wider and wider. The info-base or channel itself becomes more capable of delivering value with less effort from your team.

- You can plan to slowly integrate separate systems. Your strategy will tell you what information is most important in the existing systems. Your plan will stage the integration so that each system integrates at the proper time. Contrast this with fully integrating two systems just so that they can communicate. With a long-term integration plan, you know how to integrate only when you need to get to the information. Without the plan, you have to do massive integrations "just in case."

- You can plan to build out staff expertise over the course of years (which is how long it takes). Knowing what kind of gaps you are likely to have during the course of a 5- to 10-year plan, you can put staff on equally long training regimes. Contrast this with the approach of seeing gaps today and trying to train or hire into them immediately. Obviously, you will still have immediate needs, but by taking a longer view of staff skills, you can begin to climb out of the trap of continually having to change your skills mix. You will also breed happier, longer lasting employees if they know what you will want from them over the long term.

- You can plan which groups within your organization to work with over time. You can decide which ones are both most important to work with (i.e., have the most important information) and are easiest to work with (i.e., are the most ready to produce information in a useful way). For the groups that are important but not ready, you can plan an education program to get them ready by the time you are ready for them. (See the section titled "Proactively Approach Groups" in Chapter 11, Engage Intelligently.)

- You can plan the positioning of your unit within the organization. If you don't report to the person you should report to, what steps can you take over the next few years to reposition your group by the time you will really need it to be moved? If your group does not include other units that you feel it should, how can the acquisition of those units be staged over a number of years? Finally, how can you establish strategic, nonreporting relationships in other groups by the time you will need them in a particular project or as a liaison to another group?

- You can position projects to cover the most needs. Your strategy defines a problem space. It shows you the full range of information needs that you will someday have to meet. Each project you complete covers some amount of that space. For example, one project might cover 50 percent of the information needs of one important audience. Another might overlap 10 percent with the first but still cover the needs of several audiences. By looking at your project portfolio this way, you can specifically define projects that maximize your coverage over the short term while keeping your options open for later. (See the section titled "Problem and Solution Space" in Chapter 9, Create an Enterprise Strategy.)

 What have you done for me lately?

A **I'm glad you asked. Let me show you exactly how far we have come from the days when we just did any project that anyone asked for. We now only do projects that pay back. In the last six months, we have increased revenue by 1.5 percent, reduced expenses by 3 percent, and improved customer satisfaction by one full mark.**

Clearly, these are not all separate plans but parts of one plan that stages your takeover of the strategic information management in your organization. The interlocking plans don't have to be complex or even highly detailed. They simply need to give you a bearing on where you should be at any point in time and what to anticipate next. Of course, these plans are subject to review and revision. But notice how comprehensive your planning can be if you begin from a strong strategy.

Have an Information Perspective

Bring the executive team an information perspective. It is unlikely that anyone else on the team looks at the organization's problems as information problems. Others have their own perspectives. If you can find the information in an issue and present a concise analysis of how information can help address it, you will at least have something new to say. At most, you will have the most creative and interesting solution in the room. If you can back your analyses with a team that reliably delivers on your proposed solutions, everyone will see you consistently turn ideas into actions.

Have the research, analysis, and presentation skills of your group behind you as you make your various cases. The finance officer has pie charts and the marketing officer has glossy handouts. You can have your collected and well-organized research and recommendations presented in all the right ways too. If you don't have these skills behind you, get them.

Q **Why do your initiatives fail so often?**

A **They used to fail mostly because we did not really know why we were doing them. The technology usually worked fine, but adoption and return were always problems. Now we know exactly why we do a project, and we only do it if it is sure to be adopted. Now, when our initiatives fail (which they rarely do), it is for the right reason. Information management is damn hard, and we are forced to figure it out as we go along. We can't always get it right the first time.**

Develop analysis and organization skills to provide incisive commentary on tricky intertwined issues. Dead center in the skill terrain of information managers is organization. Good information managers are good exactly because they can take an unruly mass of information, separate out the valuable stuff, divide the good stuff into useful chunks, and relate all the chunks to each other.

The essential information management skills include:

- **Categorization** – Decide what words best describe an item of information and moreover how a system of names can be constructed that adequately describes and relates a body of content.

- **Lumping and splitting** – Lumping is deciding what items, terms, categories, and so on are really the same and need to be called the same thing. Splitting, as you can probably guess, is figuring out that a single item, term, category, and so on, needs to be broken in two.

- **Analysis, synthesis, and focus** – Look critically at a body of information, bring together seemingly diverse ideas, and focus attention on just the right information to have the desired effect.

The iSchool

Information schools are a very recent addition to academia. Some are part of a computer science department, and some are part of communications departments. All are struggling to understand and advise on information and information systems. I am part of the iSchool at the University of Washington (Seattle, Washington). Our department stands outside any wider unit, reflecting the university's view that information is a subject unto itself. The iSchool takes as its mission the integration of the more established disciplines of library science and information science with the newer realities of electronic information. Just as organizations struggle to reconcile their long-standing publication methods with the newer ones, our department struggles to wrap a definition around information that can encompass all its forms.

Information managers apply these skills every day to capture and deliver information. But having these skills gives you a fantastic tool to use in other contexts as well. For example, in a stakeholder meeting, these same skills allow you to very effectively facilitate consensus. By lumping and splitting issues, you can show stakeholders what the central issues are. Are two issues really the same? Should an issue be split because it is too big to confront? Your analysis and synthesis (especially in real time) of what people are saying are invaluable in bringing the stakeholders into the broad outlines of an agreement. By focusing attention on the central issues and away from the peripheral ones, you direct progress toward agreement. Finally, organizing issues into a taxonomy, especially for contentious groups with complex disagreements, is a great way to chart the domain of discussion as well as the broad areas of agreement and disagreement in your organization. In information management as in life, much of your success depends upon knowing when to dive into detail and when to rise into abstraction.

Be at the Center

You can be at the center of any issue whether you actually have solutions to offer. Take the stance that your group will be there to serve, whatever the executive team decides (see the Conclusion, Be the Information Guys, at the end of the book). This attitude puts you on all sides at once, removes the perception of you as an adversary or a threat, and puts you in the position of the respected general with no political agenda but a very large army behind her. Her support is assured but not taken for granted. This is not the most common approach in an executive peer group. Typically, people will opine on all issues, choose a side, and defend it.

But consider the cost of having an opinion. Is it really important that the group comes to see the problem as you do? Sometimes it is, but just as often, if not more often, your opinion is not important. What is always important is that the team comes to a unified position that can be tried and evaluated. It is also always important that you build the respect and confidence of your peers. When an issue comes along that you really need to weigh in on, they will listen and defer to you as you have deferred to them in the past.

In other words, choose your battles. Fight as few as possible and use information as a tool to mediate the rest. To meditate, use synthesis, analysis, and focus. Consider the debate on an issue to be an information base that has to be clarified, organized, and delivered back to the executive team. The more contentious the issue, the more there is a need for someone to do this work. It can be the leader of the team (the CEO, for example), but often the leader is in the fray, offering an opinion and pushing an agenda. If you can be counted on to referee, you have a guaranteed long-term position of prominence on the team. Does removing yourself from debates preclude you from coming into a position of leadership in the group? I think not. Mediation is itself a respected leadership style. Just understand that if you use mediation secretly to push an agenda, you won't be mediator for long.

Stand Up for Information

IT people are fond of structured information (that is, data). They want every bit of information to be neatly ordered in the rows and columns of their databases. The stuff they don't like dealing with cannot be stacked so neatly. They call this unstructured information or, if they want to be kind, semi-structured information. I just call it information. To them, it looks like a sprawling mess of random documents that have no consistency and no structure. In one sense, they are right. Our organizations are full of documents that are hard to categorize and impossible to break down and put in a database. In a much more important way, however, they are dead wrong. Our documents may be inconsistent and hard to categorize, but if they are worth anything at all, they are hardly unstructured. In fact, they are extremely structured.

A good document is the result of someone agonizing his or her way word by word, sentence by sentence, trying to find just the structure that will produce a desired affect. The better the information, the more carefully and artfully it is structured. It's not the kind of blatant, simplistic, and repetitive structure that you find in a database. It is a subtle, intricate structure, always converging toward a point, always logically progressing, but it is never too repetitive lest it bore us. That, by the way, is why data is so boring. You get the point after the first row, but there are 10,000 more to go. Every good document is a supremely structured entity, every word fit precisely into its sentence, every sentence a supporting beam or girder in the framework of the document's argument. I use the example of a document here, but there are all sorts of information types. A good movie, for example, has just as complicated a structure as a good book. The movie just uses a different kind of structure.

Unfortunately for someone rooted in the world of data but fortunately for normal people, the structure of each piece of handcrafted information is different. The emphasis is on interest and purpose, not conformity. As subtle as the structure within an item of information might be, the structure of the relationships between that piece and others "like" it may be even more subtle. More often than not, it is left up to the consumer to figure out how one item of information is related to others. This is generally not a problem. People have little trouble decoding the structure of well-crafted information. For information they know, they have little trouble figuring out which pieces are related to which other pieces based on whatever criteria they choose. We do this analysis all the time and without effort as the following dialogue shows:

> **Zach**: *I saw the movie* Dersu Uzala *last night.*
>
> **Corey**: *Oh yeah, that's a great one. I loved the way they structured that movie, how they superimposed the perspective of the captain on the perspective of the guide, and the way the wilderness actually became a character.*
>
> **Zach**: *Have you seen any other Kurasawa movies?*

Zach and Corey skip effortlessly from an item of information to a related one. Just try using a computer to detect structure or relate separate items, and you will see just how significant an act we perform. Unless and until the hyper-complex structure of normal information is reduced to the trivially simple structure of data, computers just can't deal with it. So, in order to allow computers to deal with the sophisticated structure of our everyday information, we use much simpler data to describe it. The computer can use this metadata (literally data about data) to encode the structure of the information as well as its relationships to other data.

What does this all mean to the information leader? It means that if you are to lead information, you will have to recognize and promote the ideas that:

- Information is not unstructured; it is hyperstructured. The complex structure of information is the very reason it is valuable. Its structure is to be preserved, not squeezed into a standard mold.

- A big intellectual effort is needed to figure out what data can be laid over the subtle structure of your information to allow it to be stored, retrieved, and delivered automatically by computers.

- An even bigger and more expensive effort is needed to review each item of information and add the appropriate data to it.

The leader of the organization's information has to stand up for information. She has to have and promote an information perspective. That perspective must be backed by a realistic plan for how information can help drive the organization toward its goals.

Chapter 8

Know the Goals

*If you don't know the goals of your organization,
you can only progress against them by chance. If you do
not know which goals are best served by information, then
you cannot design information systems that forward them.
If you can't measure progress against your goals,
then you can't know if you have served them.*

Goals are the business concerns that drive the enterprise forward. Ideally, you are part of the team that establishes and monitors goals, but at the very least you should be part of the group that is in charge of charting strategy to realize goals. However, even if you are not in charge of goals in any way, you will need to understand them fully if you hope to build systems that serve them.

Every organization has goals. Figure out what
information has to do with yours.

Let's take a commonsense approach to goals. Goals are specific statements, made by someone in authority for a unit or for the whole organization, that convey what the organization wants to achieve.

There is not much to discuss in this definition. I like to get goals from a clear authority, and I like to get them in writing so that they don't change. They don't have to apply to the entire organization to be goals, but they do have to say something that is tangible enough that you will know when the goal is met. So far, so good.

It would be nice, of course, if someone had already charted out all the significant goals, organized them, prioritized them, and delivered them to you in a usable form. Then you could get right to your real work—figuring out how information supports them. But more likely, goals are scattered about, not organized, and not prioritized. In this case, it is going to be up to you to get them into a usable form.

A friend of mine taught me a saying that is pertinent here: When you pour milk on oatmeal, all the lumps come to the top.

Your organization is the oatmeal, and your information strategy is the milk. As you produce an information strategy, you expose the lumps in your organization's goals. If your goals are lumpy when you arrive on the scene, you will have to smooth them out before you can use them.

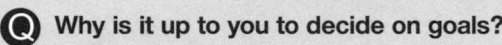

Q Why is it up to you to decide on goals?

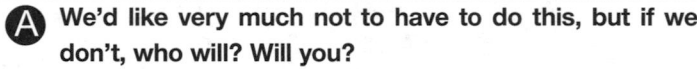

A We'd like very much not to have to do this, but if we don't, who will? Will you?

If you don't wait for someone else to figure out your goals and you succeed at organizing and rationalizing goals, you might end up with the best articulation of what the organization wants. Your goal taxonomy might just become *the* goal taxonomy. Your work may even help you turn information leadership into organizational leadership.

Defining and Selecting Goals

To define your goals, I recommend creating a goals taxonomy. Simply stated, a taxonomy is an outline. (There is a lot more to say about taxonomies, but this is not the place.) For our purposes, just imagine that a goals taxonomy is a table of contents of your organization's aims. The top levels of the outline contain goals that summarize those in the levels below. The deeper into the outline you go, the more specific the goals. There is no one way to outline your goals and, in fact, you might want to organize the same goals into different taxonomies for different purposes. For example, you can create one taxonomy of goals that outlines them by organizational unit (Finance, Operations, Human Resources, and so on) and another that organizes them by type (employee satisfaction, customer satisfaction, shareholder satisfaction, and so on). (You can try your hand at creating your goals taxonomy in the ebook Leading Information Strategy at www.laughingatthecio.com).

Expand Nationally

Sell More Product

Drive Greater Demand

Inspire More Trust in Customers

Increase Production Capacity

Importantly, just because a goal is at a higher level of this outline does not mean it is more important. For example, the goal "Inspire More Trust in Customers" may be down at level four in the taxonomy because it is naturally part of wider sales and revenue goals, while the goal "Increase Production Capacity" may be closer to the top of the taxonomy because it is logically on its own. Inspiring trust, however, may be the real key to expansion and, as such, much more important than increasing production. Taxonomies organize logically, not by importance.

That you organize goals is much more important than *how* you choose to do it. The very process of collecting goals and relating them is often enough to give you an unprecedented view of what is going on in your organization. As you work with the goals, you will find that the process of relating them is a large part of the strategy process. When you say that one goal is subsumed by another or that two goals are at the same level, you have made implicit decisions about what your current situation is and what it should be.

With a decent outline of goals, you can begin to see where to aim your systems so that they cover the most goals using the least information. You can find the goal areas that you most want to work in (uncontroversial and explicit), those that are most important to work in (highest importance and most affected by information), and those you should avoid like the plague (low importance, unaffected by information, or highly controversial).

Most importantly, you can see the entire territory that you will want to be able to speak to someday. You can plan your projects well into the future. You can understand where the biggest challenges will be and how you might attack a sub goal to get at a larger concern (like solving customer trust to drive national expansion). You can decide, for now and into the future, how high of a goal you are ready to tackle. Should you target a system at "Expand Nationally" or at "Inspire More Trust in Customers"? The former goal has higher visibility and risk but would command more resources. The latter has lower visibility and risk but is not as prestigious. (I will come back to this topic in the "Aim as High as Is Feasible" section in Chapter 9, Create an Enterprise Strategy.)

What to Know About a Goal

Simply naming goals will take you a long way toward constructing a strategy. Organizing those goals into a taxonomy that relates them will take you even further. But before you act on a goal, and especially before you commit to forwarding that goal, I suggest that you figure out the following additional information for each goal:

- **A description that fully elaborates the goal** – The name you give a goal should be designed for memorability and punch. The description should drive out any ambiguity in terms and set reasonable boundaries around the goal.

- **History and politics** – Why is this a goal of your organization? Who first proposed it? Has it been well accepted? Has there been any progress toward it? Why or why not? Who stands up for it in meetings? Who stands to win or lose if you progress toward it? Your answers might cause you to approach or avoid a particular goal.

- **Units** – What are the units of progress toward this goal? Maybe you can measure progress in dollars or in hours or some other easy unit. But maybe not. (What are the units of satisfaction or ease?) If you cannot nail down how to measure progress, you will have a hard time quantifying the amount of difference that information could make to that progress. But do not get stuck on time and money. Think hard about all the units for measuring progress.

- **Targets** – How much progress toward the goal is significant? How much progress has been made by means other than information? You need to know (or more likely negotiate) these numbers to be sure that you can sign up to deliver them.

- **Measurement** – Establishing units and targets is hard to do, but it is harder still to establish how you will measure the contribution information makes toward the goals. For example, suppose you decide that to be taken seriously by the CEO you need to raise revenue by 10 percent. You believe that by supplying the right kind of information to a particular audience, you can do that. So you put in the system to deliver the information and revenue goes up by 3.5 percent. What does that mean? What other factors affected revenue and added to or subtracted from your estimates? You will have to negotiate some ground rules for how to apportion credit and blame to the information you deliver.

Information management is still more art than science (and it may always be so). Still, if you want to be credited with progress toward your goals, you had better figure out what that means. Don't expect to be given the answers. Expect to invent them and then negotiate an agreement with your executive team to which you don't mind being held.

Chapter 9

Create an
Enterprise Strategy

As the leader of information, you must be able and willing to form simple propositions about what information should do for your organization. You must also be willing to reiterate your propositions over and over again. At some point, every conversation needs to come back to one of your propositions about what information could be doing for the organization. Use the idea of Strategy Statements to develop simple, repeatable statements about what information management you should do.

Most organizations are unclear about what information can do. Clear the clouds and simplify the conversation by balancing value with the cost of information production.

Strategy is dead center of the universe for an information leader. A clear, simple sense of what information could be doing for your organization is the most important tool in your belt. The CIO of a healthcare institution might believe that an educated (read information-consuming) customer base will be healthier. A retailer might believe that if customers knew about its great deals, they would surely buy more. The CIO of a world aid organization might contend that if potential donors only knew, they would surely give, and if leaders only knew, they would surely change policy. Whatever the sector and whatever the focus, the leader must have a firm idea of what value information brings.

From simple propositions such as these, all the details of information management practice can grow like the roots and branches of a tree. The proposition spreads roots to tap into more and more of the information implied by the proposition. It grows branches to deliver information to more and more of the people implied by the proposition. The healthcare proposition, for example, needs to plant roots into more and more sources of good information on healthy living. It needs to branch out to more and more customers whose health is in jeopardy. Like a tree, at every point in its life the information management system is self-supporting; the roots are always sufficient to support and feed the branches. Information should not be collected if it will not be delivered. The branches provide the energy to grow the entire system; the gains from the information your system already provides should justify continued investment into the further growth of the system.

As the leader of information, you must be able and willing to reiterate your propositions over and over again. At some point, every conversation needs to come back to one of your simple propositions.

"So how does this system you are proposing make our customers healthier?" the healthcare CIO might ask.

An overall strategy results from an interlocking set of these simple propositions backed by carefully staged plans that help in making the propositions operational.

My approach to strategy is simple to state. I merely ask you to answer this question:

> *What information should we deliver to which types of people to most significantly impact the goals of our organization?*

If you can come up with a good answer to this question, you will have all you need to lead both your team and executive peers. If you can prove that the impact on goals is profound, then you have all you need to lead the board as well. As your team proposes and executes projects, you can use your answers to this question to assure that they are doing the right thing. As your executive team proposes and executes enterprise strategy, you can use your answers to advise and lead. Better still, based on your strategy, you can go beyond simply supporting the plans of others and begin to directly address goals and drive the organization forward.

Before directly discussing how to answer this question, let's examine some of the conditions that determine your organization's readiness for a strategy-driven approach to information.

You Want Systems But You Need Strategy

Here is the sort of discussion I have had many times with potential clients:

> **Me:** *What can I help with?*
> **Them:** *Help us choose a system.*
> **Me:** *I can do that. Do you have a good set of requirements for the system?*
> **Them:** *We have talked to users and have a pretty long list. We also want to see what the systems can do before formalizing our requirements.*
> **Me:** *Hmm ... What sort of executive support do you have?*
> **Them:** *He's the one who told us to build the system.*
> **Me:** *Did he say why you needed to build this system?*
> **Them:** *I think it has come up over and over again at his meetings, and he finally needs to do something about it.*
> **Me:** *Hmm ... So how does this system fit into your organizational strategy?*
> **Them:** *I'm not sure what you mean.*
> **Me:** *Well, what goals is it helping you meet?*
> **Them:** *Oh, why are we doing it? Well, customers have been complaining that they can't find information. Plus, the old system is a mess; it is too hard to use so people don't contribute. Mostly, we just have too much information. We are drowning in it. We figure we can save some money and make our lives a lot easier with a new system.*
> **Me:** *Hmm ... How about audiences? I mean users. Who are the people who most need to get information from your system?*
> **Them:** *It could be anyone really. We have all sorts of people who need information.*
> **Me:** *Hmm ... What kinds of information do you think they need?*

> **Them:** *Oh, all sorts. It's all over the place, really. That's why we need a system.*
> **Me:** *Hmm … OK, how will you deliver all the information to all the people?*
> **Them:** *It will be a Web site.*
> **Me:** *Of course.*
> **Them:** *Actually, if you could just tell us what system to buy, we could skip a big selection process and get right on to implementation.*

So what is going on here? First, as best I can, let me climb into the head of the client. She is being hit from all angles: too much information, contributors unwilling to contribute, unhappy audiences, and a boss who wants something done. She knows there are products out there that say they fix all that, but she is wary. She knows that some products are better than others. They are expensive, and she wants to make the right choice. It's as simple as that.

Now let's look at the conversation from my perspective. The client is jumping into the middle of the process. Selecting a system is about halfway between concept and system roll out. Before selection comes planning, and after selection comes implementation. So the first part of the process is done, or she prefers not to do it, or she doesn't know it needs to be done. So I walk through the strategy questions that define the first phase of the project: goals, audiences, and information. The client does not seem to have established any of these three to the extent they would need to either decide if the project should be done or what project success should be based on. But then why should she have figured these things out? Her boss already told her the solution. There is no strategy to inform projects or systems. All anyone sees is the enormity of the information and an inability to manage it. I throw in the question about delivery on the off chance that "a Web site" will not be the immediate answer.

There is no one to blame here, at least unless the project fails (which it probably will). But if there were a way to apportion blame, much of it would go to the boss. The boss has issued a directive without a solid idea of why. There is no wider strategy to which the project responds, or if there is, it has not been shared with my client. In the rush to build something, knowing what groundwork is needed for success has been overlooked.

Problem and Solution Space

A simple way to position yourself between enterprise strategy on one side and projects on the other is to own the organization's information problems.

Projects lead to systems that solve those problems. To be acceptable, a project has to address one or more identified problems.

If you have done significant work on a strategy, then you know the range of problems that you are here to solve. In my strategy process, that range includes goals, audiences, and information types. These three factors form a sort of three-dimensional space of the problems that are in need of solution as the figure below describes (Figure 9.1).

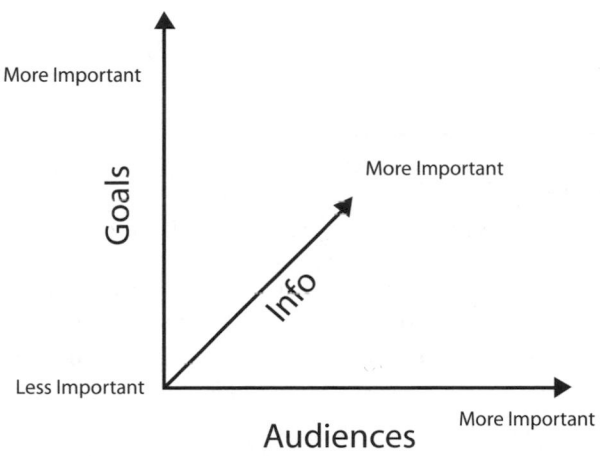

Figure 9.1 Goals, audiences, and information form a three-dimensional space into which your solutions should fall.

You can imagine your goals listed on the vertical axis with the most important ones near the top. Similarly, your audiences and information can be listed on the other two axes with more important ones farther to the right and farther into the page respectively. One goal, audience, and information type (what I call a Strategy Statement) is one point in this space. Projects cover some number of Strategy Statements, and so they are larger than single points. Eventually, you would like to cover the entire space. Existing systems cover some of the space. New projects must lead to systems that cover the rest of the space. Systems that overlap in the information dimension need to integrate somehow so they can share the information. Systems that share audiences need to be unified in their audience approach. Systems that share both information and audiences may very well be redundant.

A high-value system covers a lot of the high-value space as Figure 9.2 describes.

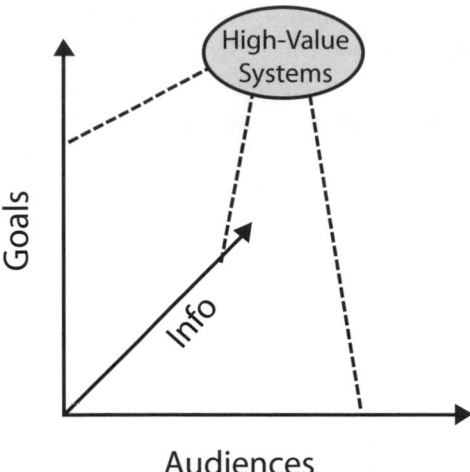

Figure 9.2 High-value systems serve high-priority goals, audiences, and information.

The system delivers high-value information to important people to meet key goals. All systems do not have to occupy this space to be worth doing, but the closer they come to this area, the more resources they should command. Systems with lower value may still be worth doing as long as they cover some of the space (as shown in Figure 9.3).

Systems that are definitely not worth doing don't cover any of the space.

This way of looking at systems helps you decide what sorts of projects need to be accomplished the most and how much of your resources they should command. For example, maybe you have large blank areas of the problem space with no project proposals pending and other parts that are crowded with proposals. What can you do to encourage projects in the blank areas?

Or maybe one project seems to be covering all the space (external Web sites are often a good example). Is there a way to break this unwieldy project into smaller ones, each with a more contained problem? Or maybe you have a predominance of projects in the low-value range and need to increase their impact on goals. If you chart your projects in this way, all sorts of possibilities will present themselves.

Value Information

No one argues against the idea that information is valuable, but it can be really hard to say exactly what that value is. You can calculate the cost of an item of information to your organization, if you have bothered to keep track of its creation or acquisition process. The item took a certain amount of handing time, which can be equated to cost. It may have required the purchase of

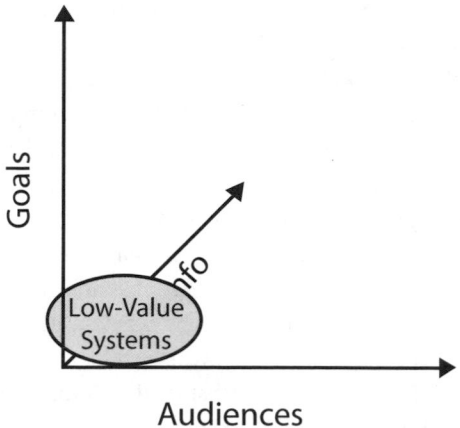

Figure 9.3   Low-value systems serve low-priority goals, audiences, and information.

software and hardware, so a portion of this capital expenditure can be assigned to the cost of the information. It may have required training and other support costs, all of which can be apportioned to the pieces of information you create. So theoretically, the cost of information can be calculated, but you probably are not organized enough to do so. Of course, any manufacturing organization that took such a casual attitude toward its product would soon be out of business. It is a fair measure of how young the Information Age is that we pay so little attention to the very asset upon which our economy is supposedly based.

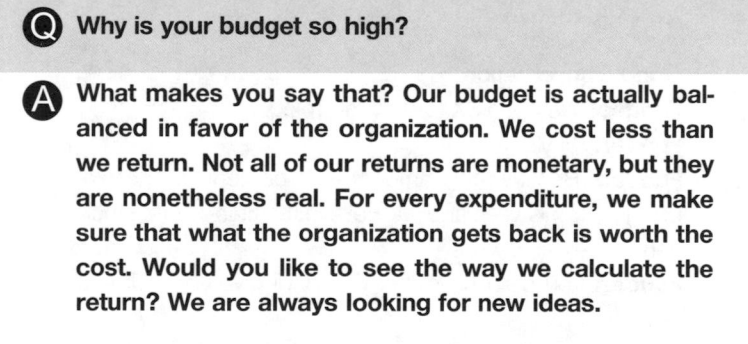

Q   Why is your budget so high?

A   What makes you say that? Our budget is actually balanced in favor of the organization. We cost less than we return. Not all of our returns are monetary, but they are nonetheless real. For every expenditure, we make sure that what the organization gets back is worth the cost. Would you like to see the way we calculate the return? We are always looking for new ideas.

In fact, whether or not we are in the Information Age, we are clearly still in the Industrial Age. We take it for granted that we have to know the cost of production for our material goods. More importantly, we have no problem assessing the value of those same goods. Subtract the cost from the value, and you know immediately if the good is worth producing. You perform valuation on material goods all the time. When you walk into a grocery store, you enter armed with a vast knowledge of what food "should" cost. You can compare two food items and decide if they are the same or different. Having determined that they are the same, you can decide if one is worth more than the other. Then you can look at the two prices and decide which one to buy.

When we are confronted with two pieces of information, the situation is quite different. Except in limited situations, we have no knowledge that allows us to assess the value of each item (and we often don't even know what an item is). We do not have enough knowledge to decide what to buy. Worse still, in most situations, we don't expect to pay for information at all. What kind of Information Age is it when we think that most information is not worth paying for?

How much funding?

How much money should you provide for a project or system?

Bad Conversation
Fundee: We need $X to do this project.
Funder: Why?
Fundee: Because that is what the software and services will cost for what we want to do.
Funder: You can't have that much, I'll give you half that amount.

Good Conversation
Fundee: We need $X to do this project.
Funder: Why?
Fundee: Because this amount is Y percent of our total budget for this year, and we believe that it is worth Y percent to deliver Z value.
Funder: You can't have that much, I'll give you half that amount.
Fundee: For that price, I can get you two-thirds of the value and not a drop more.
Funder: Two-thirds the value for half the price? I'll take it. Nice doing business with you.

How can we ever start doing information management based on value if we have no idea of the value of information? We have to find some way to measure information value. Maybe someday we will be able to say that one article, report, or service description is worth $3 while another is only worth $2. But for today, I think we have to be satisfied with less specific measures. In particular, we will have to be satisfied with a relative value. You are asking too much right now if you try to put a dollar value on an item of information. You are not asking too much if you instead ask if one type of information is more valuable than another.

Simply stated, an item (or, more generally, a type) of information is more valuable if it gets you further or faster toward your goals. A good strategy gives you the data to make this calculation. A type that serves more important goals and audiences is more valuable than one that serves fewer goals and audiences.

The units of value in this system are not necessarily dollars, so they can't always be directly subtracted from costs. Still, a strategy can provide a practical and flexible way to assign value and drive business justifications for the projects that you do.

Aim as High as Is Feasible

There are undoubtedly a lot of goals and audiences floating around your organization. Every unit and the parent of every unit all the way up to the top has goals. Every kind of person inside your organization (by department, by job, and by skills), every type of partner, and each kind of person outside that you communicate with is another potential audience. Which ones should you choose to include in your strategy? It could be suicidal to reach too far. Reach not far enough and you risk irrelevance. Rather than guess at how far to reach, take a cool-headed approach based on the maturity of your team and organization.

First, consider the maturity of your team. You might be in any one of these general situations:

- **Just getting started** – Maybe you were just put in charge of a set of previously separate units, maybe your team has been focused on data and infrastructure management previously, maybe you are in a new organization, or maybe you just have not gotten information management off the ground.

- **A lot to prove** – Maybe your group is in a position of weakness because of a string of visible failures. The organization does not understand what you do. Maybe your very position as leader is in jeopardy, and the idea of information management is discredited or unknown in your organization.

- **Heading up** – Maybe you have had a recent success (in overhauling a Web site perhaps). The organization is provisionally behind you, but it is now looking for you to take on more and more information management. Maybe you have the ear but not the heart of the executive team. You still have something to prove, but the assumption of success is yours.

- **Consolidating** – Maybe you are firmly established with the organization and the executive team. Maybe you have most of the skills you need and are now looking to institutionalize information management as a way of doing business.

- **Really leading** – Maybe information management is considered as important as any of the other major functions. You have a firmly established information strategy and a string of successful projects. Your team can handle the tactics and most of the strategy setting. Maybe you are ready to assert your leadership beyond information.

Next, consider the maturity of your wider organization. How well-established and organized are its goals and its understanding of whom it serves? Is there a comprehensive, vetted hierarchy of goals, or are the goals undocumented and unrelated? Is there a comprehensive audience analysis out there? Does it span internal as well as external audiences, or are audiences only something that the marketing (or public relations) department cares about, are not generally agreed upon and are relatively unknown in the rest of the enterprise? These qualities are summarized in Figure 9.4.

In the "Low Team Maturity/Low Goals & Audience Maturity" quadrant, neither your team nor your organization is ready to do a real information strategy. In this case, you had better just prove that a strategic approach to information is possible. Choose an uncontroversial goal and audience, and then plan to deliver just enough information to the audience to assure clear progress against the goal. In addition, work to increase your team's strength and begin to organize the goals of your organization into an actionable taxonomy. You are best served in this quadrant by staying pre-strategic in your projects while you get ready for strategy.

In the "High Team Maturity/High Goals & Audience Maturity" quadrant, on the other hand, you have everything you need to squeeze maximum benefit out of the information in your organization. You can use the already existing goals and audience analysis to generate a comprehensive strategy. The strategy can chart the goals that cross audiences to show who is really

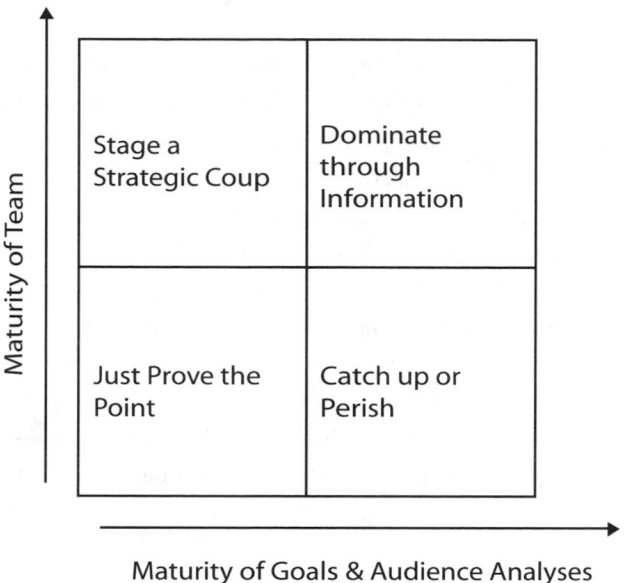

Maturity of Goals & Audience Analyses

Figure 9.4 I am loath to do so, but the situation calls for a four-quadrant diagram.

most critical to your success. It can chart information across goals and audiences to show exactly which information carries the highest value. If you are in this quadrant, you are lucky indeed, but your life will be tough as you reach for the golden ring of information management—a comprehensive integrative strategy that finally establishes information as a prime mover of the organization.

The "Low Team Maturity/High Goals & Audience Maturity" quadrant—straight down from the dizzying heights of "High/High"—is the area of highest risk to you. The organization is ready, but you are not. You may be lucky. The organization may not know it has everything you need to transcend your current narrow focus but don't depend on it. More and more information leaders are taking a fall for not being able to get their teams to do what everyone now knows they should do.

If I were in this quadrant, I would pull the plug on any project that could make my team's position even worse. I would gather the best of my staff and make sure I could generate a short-term success against what the organization has defined as top goal and audience. I would look outside for technical, managerial, and analysis talent to plug the gaps in my team while I build. Finally, before anyone above me in the organization began asking questions, I would go on the offensive, promoting the vision of good information management and looking for support to build my team around the vision. In other words, I would lead with strategy while backfilling talent and process as quickly as possible.

The "High Team Maturity/Low Goals & Audience Maturity" quadrant is my favorite. In this situation, your team is ready, but the organization is not. You are primed to do strategic information management, and your highly skilled and amply staffed team could be initiating a wealth of strategically significant projects if only you could figure out what was most important to do. It may be time for a "Coup de Gestion," a management takeover. What would happen if, in order to do your job, you took the lead on figuring out the goals and audience it is most important to serve? What if you did a great job of this? What if the way you crossed the goals of the organization with its constituencies provided a fresh and new way to grasp what the organization was doing, and more importantly, what it should do? What if suddenly no one in the organization had a better idea of what was going on and what to do next? I'll let you decide.

Make Strategy Statements

Strategy Statements link the three most important information management elements. I created the idea of Strategy Statements to try and boil information management down to simple memorable statements of the form:

> *By delivering <information> to <audience> we will be better able to <goal> because <justification>*

Each Strategy Statement describes one inarguably good thing you can do with your information. This Strategy Statement is no more than a restatement of the question that I base all strategy on: What information should we deliver to which types of people to significantly impact the goals of our organization? The crucial differences are:

- In the Strategy Statement, there are slots for named goals, audiences, and information. You have to be specific.

- A brief justification is required. Simply stating that there is a relationship between delivering information and meeting goals is not as good as proving it.

- There can be any number of these Strategy Statements. There can also be sub-Strategy Statements that further refine and extend the more general statements.

With a little work, these simple statements can form the basis of a comprehensive information strategy. Forming a short, sharp statement about what to do is a great way to get clear yourself. Armed with a crisp statement, you can begin to win others over. As you explore the terrain of statements that are undeniably true, they begin to connect. The same ideas come up again and again. As you go even further, the simple statements begin to form a comprehensive landscape, and you are on your way to an information strategy.

Strategy Statements are a powerful tool. With one Strategy Statement, you can design a convincing business case for a project. With a comprehensive set of Strategy Statements that spans your most important goals and audiences, you have a basis for a full information strategy. If a proposal can't be related to a Strategy Statement, then either you need a new Strategy Statement or the proposal is not justified.

You can build a strategy from an interconnected set of Strategy Statements that cover all the most important goals of your organization. They state, as specifically as possible, how information delivered to people can help you meet your goals. This method is deceptively simple. You just list a set of goals, decide what people are needed to meet those goals, and then decide what information will encourage them to help you meet your goal. The first difficulty comes in naming and organizing all the goals, audiences, and information types. The real difficulty comes in making a simple justification that intuitively links audiences and information to a goal. The final hurdle is getting those around you to behave in accordance with your formulation.

In an ideal world, you would have the entire organization participating in the creation of Strategy Statements. In the real world, you may have to begin alone. I hope you can at least recruit some of your more enlightened staff to help you. When you get comfortable with the process, you might also begin to draw in some of your peers. The nice thing about the Strategy Statements is that they can be done on the back of a napkin by someone who knows nothing about information management.

As a general process, you might follow these broad steps:

1. **Play first** – Before getting serious, be sure to try out the process on a lot of napkins and whiteboards.

2. **Make a high-level pass** – Before working through to a complete analysis, work at a global level. Choose big, easy-to-understand goals, well-known audiences, and clearly important information (for example, "By delivering compliance documentation to regulators we can keep our CEO out of jail").

3. **Revise iteratively** – Make multiple passes through the analysis, each time deepening it one level and interrelating your statements.

When you finally get down to the lowest level of details, the result should be an efficient system of highly interconnected Strategy Statements. At each iteration, pit your own ideas and analysis against the best wisdom of key people in your organization, and then think hard about how to synthesize the two.

A full process for forming Strategy Statements and strategy is presented in the ebook Leading Information Strategy at www.laughingatthecio.com. Here I will just summarize the process.

A Sample Strategy Statement

In Table 9.1, I have listed a part of the Strategy Statement analysis that Allied Financial Systems (AFS) might have done (see Part 1, Laughing at the CIO).

Table 9.1   A Small Part of a Strategy Statement Analysis

Goal	Audience	Information
Establish more relationships	Customers	Industry Backgrounders
Establish more relationships	Customers	Layman Product Descriptions
Establish more relationships	Customers	Staff Profiles
Establish more relationships	Customers	Competition Smack-Downs
Establish more relationships	Customers	Questions and Answers

The Strategy Statements you might derive from this analysis are as follows:

- By delivering Industry Backgrounders to Customers, we will establish more relationships. The backgrounders will help the customer sort out what they want from us, focus their questions, and establish our credibility.

- By delivering Layman Product Descriptions to Customers, we will establish more relationships. The descriptions will help the customer sort out our product offerings, focus their questions, and establish our credibility.

- By delivering Staff Profiles to Customers, we will establish more relationships. The profiles will help them get comfortable with their salesperson and choose an analyst with whom they can bond.

- By delivering Competition Smack-Downs to Customers, we will establish more relationships. The smack-downs will help customers decide in favor of us over the competition.

- By delivering Questions and Answers to Customers, we will establish more relationships. They will help move customers past their confused state and onto the ability to commit.

Establishing more customer relationships is something AFS wants to accomplish. This goal happens to be part of a wider goal of national expansion. You can imagine that there are other sub-goals that also support this larger goal. Also, there may be other larger goals that the goal of more customer relationships supports as well (raising revenue, for example). At any rate, the information leader has decided to focus on this goal because he suspects that information can help AFS reach it.

Customers are obviously critical to getting AFS to this goal. The customers have to want to establish the relationships or they will not happen. So how do you get potential customers to want to start a relationship? According to the Strategy Statement, if customers feel "safe, comfortable, and well served from the first interaction," they will begin more relationships. That is not the only way to get customers to engage, but it is clearly one way. The logic here is simple: If customers feel comfortable, they will engage. If the leader finds other ways to get customers to engage, he can form other Strategy Statements. Similarly, if different kinds of customers have different triggers for engaging, then the leader can break this broad audience category into smaller ones, each with its own Strategy Statements.

The kinds of information listed should all contribute to making customers feel safer, more comfortable, and well served. If they do contribute, then these types of information will also contribute to the larger goal of forming more relationships. When you break information into types and give each type a memorable name, an interesting thing happens. Rather than thinking about information as a continuous undifferentiated mass (like when you say "we need to supply customers with comforting information"), the names force you to think very specifically about information. It turns information into different kinds of objects that you can imagine creating, storing, and delivering. Naming types is the first big step to making information manageable.

I cover the idea of informant types in much more detail in Chapter 5, Work Through Information, of the ebook Leading Information Strategy at www.laughingatthecio.com.

For each row in Table 9.1, one Strategy Statement is listed. Here, too, the logic should be simple:

> *By delivering Staff Profiles to Customers, we will establish more relationships. The profiles will help them get comfortable with their salesperson and choose an analyst with whom they can bond.*

The argument should sound straightforward and reasonable on its face. Others in the organization may agree or disagree with it, but they cannot fail to understand it. In the usual course of events, there should be lots of debate about the efficacy of this Strategy Statement. People can argue with the logic, or they can argue that there are information types that would better meet the goal. Those are arguments you want to have. By putting forward a Strategy Statement with a simple and immediately graspable logic, you have provided just the right forum for debate. The Strategy Statement that emerges from the debate will also have to be just as understandable and reasonable. Spend less time assuring that your first Strategy Statements are right and more time assuring that they frame the coming debate in a productive way.

In the end, the Strategy Statements you turn into strategy should be true and important. Their logic should be unassailable and their impact on the goal should be significant. You should be able to take the information types specified in the Strategy Statements and begin to build the process and technology for delivering them to the audience. You should be able to quantify the types. What is a Staff Profile composed of? How many will we need to create? How often do they change?

The Strategy Statements also take you to the heart of the rhetoric of information as well as its type. Rhetoric is persuasion (as I mention in "Information Persuades" in Chapter 6, Know Why Information Matters). Making customers feel more comfortable is an act of persuasion. The content of a Staff Profile, not simply the delivery of it, is what will persuade. So in addition to the easy questions about "who" and "how much," you need to start asking the much harder questions about the arguments, credibility, context, argument, narrative, and style. Even something as seemingly data-like as a staff profile is essentially a persuasive communication.

Of course, information management can't do everything. No matter how persuasive the information is that you deliver, customers may remain uncomfortable for reasons beyond your control. If the attitude of the salesperson, the press AFS has received, comments from the competition, or a thousand other factors make the customer fearful, then all the persuasive information you deliver will be regarded as so much propaganda. You can't control these outside factors, but you can consider them. Ask yourself, "What outside factors might render our information less valuable?" If you think that there is a fair chance of those outside factors intervening, then maybe you should choose another type of information that is more immune to these factors.

One small goal matched with one audience yielded five Strategy Statements. Clearly, there are many Strategy Statements needed to fully elaborate your strategy. Once again, information management shows itself to be a lot of work. You can cut this work down drastically by making sure to surface a small set of audiences and information types that impact the largest set of goals. If you do a good job on your Strategy Statements, you will have the tools to contain the explosion of information in the rest of your organization.

A Simple Strategy Statement Exercise

You can make the process of generating and linking Strategy Statements as official as you want. You can assign project management, canvass widely for input, and have stakeholder "smack-down" sessions where you work together through to the final product. Regardless of how official or casual your process is, however, actually generating Strategy Statements can be fairly simple. In this section, I'll walk you through that process. You can use it to do Strategy Statements yourself or do them jointly with a small group. You can also show the process to a wide range of people, let them all use it, and then collect, collate, and review the results.

Find Goals

To begin, in Table 9.2, simply list the top three goals of your organization along with a justification explaining why this goal is important enough to make your list.

Before you go on, pause for a moment. Do you fully understand and embrace these goals? If you don't really understand them, now is a good time to get with the executive program and find out all you can about these drivers. If you don't support one or more of these goals, maybe you should choose others who you do support. And, of course, the big question to ask yourself is:

Do you really think that information can get you closer to these goals?

Table 9.2 The Top Three Goals Information Can Address

	Goal	Justification
1.		
2.		
3.		

If information can get you closer, how much closer? Remember that whatever you do will probably cost a lot of money, so the impact you make on a goal had better be significant. If you don't know whether information can impact these goals, keep going. By the end of this exercise, you should at least be able to come up with something to start with.

Relate Goals to Audiences

From the three goals you came up with, choose one with which to continue. Use the one that you feel can best be advanced by delivering information to particular people. You may not think of your customers, members, employees, constituents, or users as audiences, but don't worry about that right now. Look back at your top goal and decide on three types of people who are most pivotal to your organization meeting this goal (Table 9.3).

As with the goals, give each audience a good name and a justification that states how they support your goal. Try to put yourself in their shoes and decide what actions or thoughts on their part will get you closer to your goal. Think hard and be sure you understand your justification. For the purposes of

Table 9.3 The Top Three Audiences for the Top Goal

	Audience	Justification
1.		
2.		
3.		

this exercise, these people are the means to your ends (but not outside this exercise, please). In the next step, you will decide what information to give them based on how you think they can help you reach your goal. For now, think hard about what you want them to think, believe, or do to help you reach your goal. I'll cover audiences in much more detail in the "Shift Audience Ownership" section in Chapter 10, Devolve Ownership.

At this point in the exercise, you have decided who is most pivotal to the success of your organization. These people may not be the ones you ultimately end up serving information to, but they are definitely the ones you want to serve, if possible. Now, take a hard look. Can you move these people with information? If not, go on to other audiences or maybe even other goals. Are there so few of them that you are better off giving them a call rather than building them a system? If so, go on to other audiences. If you are still lost and have no idea if or how information can move these people to think or do what you need them to, you have one more section to figure it out. But first, go back to what you want them to do or think. What does that have to do with information? On the other hand, I'm hoping that some light bulbs are beginning to appear over your head. I'm hoping that you are already seeing some obvious connections between goals and audiences that are mediated by information.

Relate Goals and Audiences to Information

Up until now, you could have been doing a marketing exercise. But you are not doing marketing, you are doing information. To finish the exercise, take one audience for the goal you chose earlier and decide on three types of information you can deliver to help (persuade, provide incentives, etc.) them help you meet your goal (Table 9.4).

As always, be careful to choose a good name. This name may be a bit harder than the others if you are not used to naming information types. Try to

Table 9.4   The Three Most Important Information Types for One Audience and Goal

	Information	Justification
1.		
2.		
3.		

avoid saying "Information about …" Give it a try and be prepared to work your names over a few times before they are ready to be used in conversation.

The justification should follow naturally from the justification you created for how the audience impacts your goal. For example, suppose the goal is a national expansion, and single women are key because you expect them to be the first adopters of your services. Figure out what information will help them be those first adopters and why the information type you chose will particularly do that.

Try to come up with justifications that are so obvious that no one in your organization could possibly disagree. If you can't create such a simple justification, reconsider this information type or even the audience or goal that led you to it. The value of this exercise lies precisely in the simplicity of your logic. If you can't find at least one goal and audience that is incontrovertibly served by information, how will you ever justify an entire strategy?

The Finished Strategy Statements

You should now have all you need to make three pithy, powerful statements about what your information management systems should do in the form:

> *By delivering <information> to <audience> we will be better able to <goal> because <reason>.*

Review your completed Strategy Statements and ask yourself if they hang together. Are you convinced that if you could somehow deliver this sort of information to these sorts of people, your organization would necessarily move a significant distance forward toward the goal? What further support for this argument would you need to make the case unassailable? The way I designed the exercise, whatever you come out with should be important enough to do, but stop and consider. If it came to pass that these people got your information and did what you wanted, how big of a deal would it be for your organization?

Next, ask yourself how understandable the statement is. Would someone get it at a first hearing? Is the vocabulary unfamiliar? Do you need to have some background knowledge before you could fathom the relationships you have made? Try saying the Strategy Statement to a few people and see how they respond. Work with the language to increase the lucidity and impact of the statement.

Finally, ask yourself how doable this Strategy Statement is. Can you clearly envision collecting this sort of information and getting it in a usable form to the audiences? If your Strategy Statement makes it past all these barriers, it is ready to be used as is, or interrelated with other Strategy Statements to form a complete strategy.

In this exercise, you have crafted three Strategy Statements for one goal and one audience. With all three goals and all three audiences times three information types, you could have as many as 27 Strategy Statements at your fingertips. I think you can see both the great potential of this method as well as the challenge of keeping it under control. Of course, many of the Strategy Statements you come up with will not pan out. Other Strategy Statements, however, will present themselves as you think of new goals, audiences, and information types. But for now, you should be happy to have at least three rock-solid, understandable, sound, and doable Strategy Statements.

I'm hoping that by doing this brief exercise, you have gotten a good taste for what it means to lead information. The Strategy Statements you arrived at are a clear expression of three important things your organization should do with information. Anyone who comes to you with a reasonable proposal for how to turn this strategy statement into a working system should be welcomed. Anyone who comes to you with a different project proposal should be prepared to back it up with reasoning at least this strong. When your boss asks you what you are doing and why you belong at the strategic level of the enterprise, you can trot out these and other statements that, first, show that you know how to think strategically, and, second, that you have specific and important ideas of how to make information central to the success of your organization.

Go Top-Down and Bottom-Up

To be sure your strategy is right, you need to drive it from both directions. The Strategy Statements method I describe has a basic top-down skeleton onto which substance can be added from the bottom-up. The top-down skeleton works from the goals of the organization to the information (and later the information systems) that you need. The bottom-up substance you can add to this skeleton includes:

- **Input from stakeholders** – People at every level of the organization can tell you about goals, audiences, and information. The advice you get from the audience-facing staff is often the best you will receive.

- **Review of systems** – Systems now in place might be serving an important information type to important people. What do these systems tell you about the wider strategy you should pursue?

- **Competitive analysis** – What sorts of information and audiences are other organizations working with? If you spend some time looking at your peers or competitors, you add validation and depth to your strategy analysis.

I provide an overview of a method for competitive analysis in the ebook Leading Information Departments at www.laughingatthecio.com.

If your strategy is to succeed, you will need to integrate the ideas you derive logically from goals with the ideas that bubble up from the large base of people and other organizations you will come in contact with. If your organization is ready, you can take the next step and drive the strategy process out of your team and into the rest of the organization. Just like budgets percolate up and down through the organization, matching local needs to global realities, your information strategy can do the same. Unfortunately, few organizations are really ready to do strategy on this scale. Until then, you and your team can combine a Strategy Statement Analysis with input from below to build a preliminary strategy.

Chapter 10

Devolve Ownership

*Once you have firmly established your ownership of
information management, act quickly to spread that
ownership to the rest of the organization. Continue to
lead the enterprise, but shift strategy creation and updates
to the business units and move ownership of audiences
and information to the people who know them best.*

The point of acquiring ownership of information management is to get it
off the ground and organized. Once it is going, it is in your best interest and
the interest of the organization to pass that ownership on. For you, ownership
represents an enormous amount of work that you will not want to continue to
do. For the organization at large, distributed strategy ownership makes for a
better strategy.

Continue to stay ahead of and direct your organization. However, make sure that
others take more ownership of the strategy and management load.

When you own the strategy, you tell groups what they want from you. When groups own their own strategy, they tell you directly what they want. When you own the strategy, you decide if the projects deliver value. When groups own their own strategy, they decide if your projects deliver value.

Your client groups will judge your value with or without a strategy. A strategy gives you the tool you need to make sure that both you and they use the same judgment criteria.

Shift Strategy Ownership

The CFO does not craft the budget for every business unit. Instead, she gives them baselines and constraints. Then she takes all the budgets crafted by units and synthesizes them into a budget for the organization. You could do the same. The CFO responds to, critiques, and pushes back on the individual budgets, trading economic necessities off each other. You could do this as well. You could trade information management necessities off each other and massage the strategies of each business unit into the strategy for the organization as a whole. You could do all this if only you could count on the leaders of those business units to put together a strategy. But, of course, you can't. All managers know (and many dread) that they must put together a budget periodically. They know that their success hinges on doing it right, and they put a lot of effort into it. No manager I know thinks this way about information.

But could they think this way? Why not? If we are really becoming an information economy, won't they have to? Someday, if information is anywhere near as valuable as money, an information strategy will be a standard deliverable for all managers and executives. Until that day, it may remain up to you to push the idea. But even today, you can bring your strategy out to other groups to validate and hone it. Along the way, you can begin to build relationships with the leaders of these groups. Your relationships with the groups that are the most important to the strategy can be founded on the same terms as is your strategy itself.

For example, if your strategy states that delivering investment tips to new customers of your financial services is a good way to increase transaction volume, then the analyst groups that have tips are a prime group to approach. Even if they don't produce tips now and have little relationship to current information systems, theirs is a key relationship to build. Eventually, you might like them to figure out how the information they hold can impact transaction volume and other goals, but at first, simply telling them that they hold strategic information may be all you can do. Over time, and with particularly savvy people and groups, you can begin to delegate to others ownership of the strategy. In the long run, if having an information strategy is worth the effort, groups will do it. It's just not clear how long the run will be.

There is one lever you can pull today to get groups to consider strategy: Make the approval of a project they want you to do contingent on establishing its strategic value. You can make your strategy a bar to get over to get a project on the schedule (as I describe in "Boot Up a Strategic Project Evaluation Process" in Chapter 16, Lead Information Projects). The first time a group confronts this barrier, express to them that if they take part in crafting the strategy, their projects are sure to be in line with it. Most units are not ready to craft information strategy. The ideas they have about the value of their systems are based on other criteria, and while their criteria may be fine within their group, your criteria, as established by the strategy, are good for the entire organization. Your criteria put their projects in a wider context and promote a general rise in the value of information and information systems throughout the organization. By buying into your wider system of value criteria, other groups are assuring that their investment in information returns as much as possible for the entire organization. For example, the analyst group I mentioned above may be pushing you to create an intranet for their group. The intranet may deliver value to the analyst group (if they have done their homework), but what does it do for the company? Moreover, does it do more or less for the company than collecting and delivering tips? With a strategy, you can decide. Equally importantly, your strategy can be an external arbiter that makes negotiations over value and resources fair and less political.

Information strategy is built from an analysis of goals, audiences, and information. Goals are the easiest to delegate to others. Any unit can tell you what it wants to accomplish. Aligning its goals with those of peers and the larger organization (a job you would think each unit would have already done) can be tough. Still, there are not a lot of goals, and goals are neither terribly complex nor prone to sudden change. So the work you do to codify and organize goals need not be burdensome. Once you have gotten other groups to take charge of their own goals, you can begin to work on audiences and information, which are considerably tougher to pass off.

Shift Audience Ownership

Who should ultimately own the definition of the most important audiences for your information? Before you reflexively answer "marketing" or "public relations" or even "corporate communications," consider your audiences. For our purposes, an audience is a group of people who by receiving information can help you meet a goal. At the highest level, these audiences can be separated into the following categories:

- **Internal** – People within your organization. In addition to divisions by job type, there are possible divisions by unit, discipline, organizational level (management, executive, professional, and so on), location, and a host of other attributes.

- **Partner** – People in your value or supply chain. You work with them more or less closely in ways that meet the goals of your organization and theirs. There are as many ways to subdivide this general category as there are kinds of partner relationships.

- **External** – People outside your organization. They may be customers, members, patrons, constituents, or those in a vast number of other relationships with your organization.

Your marketing and public relations unit usually cares only about the third type of audience. Your corporate communications unit might do some work in the first two categories, but it is not enough to make them want to fully own the analysis. You might be in one of the few fortunate organizations with a department that is the natural owner of a full-audience analysis but probably not.

Your group may have to be the one that owns the definitive audience analysis for your organization. That does not mean other groups cannot own parts of it. Marketing, for example, will likely insist on owning the definitive customer analysis. That's fine. As long as they don't mind including you in their process so you can merge their analysis with all the others you have to integrate, all is well. Whatever other units hold a piece of the analysis (if you have any) can do the same.

Your job (in the beginning as well as in the long run) can be to mediate between the groups who serve the same audience and to operationalize the idea of audiences into an audience model that can be used within projects.

There is more on audience modeling in the ebook Leading Information Strategy at www.laughingatthecio.com. Also, the fullest audience modeling coverage is in the Content Management Bible at cmbible.com.

Get Audiences Out of Projects

Your project teams probably do a lot of great work to understand their audiences. Unfortunately, that knowledge and respect for audiences often remains in the project team and never moves into other projects that could use it. Any audience modeling the project team creates remains within the business logic and database schemas of the systems they create.

If an audience is truly important to the organization's success, then the relationship with that audience should be understood, analyzed, and codified outside of any particular project. Marketing knows this well. The people who create a campaign, flyer, or commercial are not the ones who figure out what is needed from an audience. They get this information when their project begins. If they advance the understanding or approach of an audience during their project, their creativity is shared with the other teams who approach the same audience.

So why is audience analysis, profiling, and personalization so often considered a job for information architects and other professional staff within projects? Under the headings of user analysis, user-centered design, usability, user experience, etc., audience analysis is done and redone in project after project. Why doesn't this analysis precede and supersede the project it is used in?

I'm not saying that information architects and other project staff should not do this work. In fact, I think they do a great job of it. Traditional marketing professionals have much to learn from information architects (who could learn a thing or two from a good marketer as well). I simply believe that the work we do to analyze audiences should be done outside and beyond particular projects. Audience analysis is an enterprise function. It should be well funded and performed well once (perhaps by the same information architects that have been trapped within projects). The relevant parts of the analysis should be given to the project team at the start of the project. Project teams should have the power to critique the audience analysis they are given and drive it further when they apply it.

This approach does not take any more total effort than you are expending now to understand audiences in individual projects. In fact, depending upon how much redundancy there is across projects, it might take less. More importantly, it coordinates your efforts and develops an ever deepening, shared understanding of the kind of people who matter most to your organization's success.

Practice Audience Stewardship, Not Proprietorship

It would be nice if someone in the organization had done the work of audience analysis for you and could deliver an accurate, working audience model to your project teams. On the other hand, you are doing a lot of work already to understand and model audiences, so maybe your group is the logical place for this analysis to live. It may not be hard for you to coalesce the work that has been done to understand audiences and turn it into a shared model that project teams can draw from.

As an aside, a shared audience model is the best backbone you can create for sharing information. Two systems that serve the same audience and use the same model for deciding what information to provide are easy to integrate.

Even if your group ends up owning the overall audience model, it should be more stewardship than proprietorship. Your group's central role should be to organize, care for, and distribute the information, and to not decide who the most important audiences are. Still, you can do a lot to forward the process by collecting audience information from these sorts of stakeholders:

- **Audience** – Members of the audience can speak for themselves.

- **Authors** – The people who create the information for an audience should have a special understanding of that audience and a stake in how the audience is served.

- **Audience professionals** – Writers, editors, producers, and others who make a living specifically studying and shaping information for audiences have the credentials to speak for an audience and have a stake in how the audience is approached.

- **Concerned units** – Units within your organization that directly depend on an audience for help, revenue, or any other form of support have a stake in how the organization approaches that audience.

- **Representatives** – Groups or individuals that congregate the audience (professional organizations, departments were they all work, elected officials, and so on) are great sources of information about an audience, and they have a stake in how that audience is served by your organization.

If your team has such people, they should contribute to the audience analysis. In any case, however, your team must find these sorts of stakeholders and get them to contribute. Then your team must mediate the disagreements and terminology discrepancies between different stakeholders who speak for the same audience.

Shift Information Ownership

Most groups have an ad-hoc and lackadaisical attitude toward the information that they produce. They have never looked closely at it. They could not tell you what types they have let alone what goals the information addresses and its relative values. They have no plans for investing in information based on its ability to return value. In short, they don't take information very seriously.

If you can get units to take their information seriously and treat it as an enterprise asset, you will be well on your way to enlisting them to own their own information strategy. As a unit begins to get serious about its information, the unit is led naturally and directly to the wider concerns of audiences and goals.

Getting serious about information mostly means taking ownership for its proper creation and maintenance. In addition to spurring the unit to own strategy, there is a much more practical reason why you need to get groups to fully own their information. You can't continue to accumulate staff responsibilities as you do projects. If you do, you will soon find yourself at the head of an enormous editorial team with a workload and production schedules that are decided by a hundred different managers, none of whom are in your own group.

To avoid this ever-escalating editorial burden, you need to pass off editorial responsibilities as they arise. Responsibility for the creation and quality of information authored or acquired by a group needs to lie with that group by the time any system that uses that information is launched. As soon after a system launches as possible (or before), the groups that supply information should plan to provide all the staff that touches the information.

Modeling information is much harder to pass off and will likely remain a core service of your group.

I discuss information modeling further the ebook Leading Information Strategy at www.laughingatthecio.com.

Take Information Seriously

A change in information ownership is good for your group, and it is also good for contributors. It gives them the opportunity (or forces them) to get the most from their information. Because information production is so expensive, the group is forced to consider the return on their investment. They are drawn by necessity into value calculations on their information. They are encouraged to withdraw support for information that does not bring them value and invest more heavily in information that does. It's good medicine. But unfortunately that is how it tastes to many groups: They are forced to confront the entire can of information management worms when they might prefer to get less value but pay nothing.

The central problem with devolving information ownership is a big one:

> *The benefits of information management do not always accrue to the suppliers of that information.*

Take the example of an engineering group. Suppose there is information in the minds of the engineers that customers really want. What value does it bring the engineers to spend the time it takes to say what they know, let alone create well-formed items of the information types you need? Not much. The real beneficiaries are in the sales unit where the engineers' information brings in new customers. Not only does information production fail to bring engineers value, it costs them dearly. Information production is especially expensive for people who are not good communicators.

If information is important, then someone accrues value from its production. The challenge is to assure that enough benefits accrue to the contributors to offset their costs of production. In business terms, the equation is simple. The information has some cost (borne by the contributors), and it has some value (accrued by someone). If the value exceeds the cost, then there is a reason to produce it. If the cost accrues to one group but the benefit accrues to another, then the group that profits should in some way commission the creators. None of this need be monetary. For example, the value might be measured in units of customer satisfaction and the cost in units of recognition. How much customer satisfaction is worth the cost of recognizing the contributors?

In the example of the engineers, there are a number of ways to approach and overcome the cost/value disparity:

- First, the project of collecting and distributing information can be owned high enough in the organization to span both the information contributors and the recipients of benefits. In that way, the owners can control both sides of the equation. In this example, there may be quite a distance between the engineering and sales groups. The ownership might climb all the way to the executive level. Interestingly, this wide separation between contributors and beneficiaries is common. Information flow often has no relationship to organizational structure.

- Second, particular benefits can accrue to the contributors to offset their increased responsibilities. If the information is really valuable, this should not be hard to do. In the case of the engineers, maybe a percentage of the increased sales could be directly funneled into new test equipment. Of course, to do this, you would have to be able to quantify exactly how much sales increased because of the engineers' information, which is a great exercise. Recognition and nonmaterial rewards are more common forms of returned value than money. The engineers could have their job descriptions modified to include creation of this information. Their supervisors could review them on it, and salary and promotion decisions could be based upon it. Again, if the information is demonstrably valuable and the project owners have a span of control that includes the managers of the engineers, then this should be possible. Of course, if the engineers and their managers have no consciousness of the value of information, then they will resist any moves to "make" them produce information.

- Finally, the organizational structure can adjust to accommodate the increased responsibilities of the contributors. For example, when confronted with the prospect of getting engineers to type, the organization might instead contract a group of writers to interview the engineers and transcribe what they say. The added cost and indirectness of the information creation would presumably be offset by the higher quality of the text and reduced stress on the engineers.

If you want a unit to take its information seriously, you will need to help them adjust to the change. Education and encouragement go a long way (as I mention in the "Form an Education Plan" section in Chapter 11, Engage Intelligently). In the end, however, the unit will support or resist you based on its own internal calculations of the effort it puts out and the value it receives.

Produce Reusable Information

In addition to owning the production of information, originating groups should take increasing responsibility for producing information in a way that is generally useful. This may be as simple as having them use a style guide in their word processor or as complex as having contributors learn an intricate document model and author in XML. The method is not as important as the concept. Today's information creators cannot be as casual as those of the past.

Producing useful information includes:

- **Creating information in a structured way** – To be useful, information has to have a known and standard structure. For example, each case study might need a title, an abstract, a situation analysis, and a conclusion. If all case studies are structured this way, they are easy to automatically display. If they are all different, your options for storage and display become severely limited.

- **Communicating with multiple audiences** – Contributors must know the possibly wide range of people who might consume their work and be able to communicate effectively with all of them. This might require them to write more generally or create multiple independently targeted versions of the same information.

- **Writing in useful chunks** – Contributors must segment their information into pieces that can be appropriately targeted and delivered to particular audiences with particular information needs. For example, rather than producing a single 50-page report, a contributor might need to produce 10 interconnected five-page chunks that can be delivered separately or together.

- **Metatagging** – In addition to producing information, today's authors must categorize their information as well. Categorizing is a different skill than creating information. To create information, you need to know about a subject matter. To categorize, you need to know how your information relates to the rest of the information that others have created.

- **New tools** – Contributors are often accustomed to using only one sort of tool to create information (a word processor, for example). Today, there are all sorts of new tools to create and tag information.

People have been able to get away with the idea that they create information however they want, for whomever they want, and structure it in whatever way occurs to them. Groups that produce information need to lose these freewheeling ways for the more standardized and sophisticated ways of modern information management. If they do not rise to this challenge and still want good systems, then someone else (your team, perhaps?) will have to do this work for them.

The additional challenge of creating reusable information stops many units from taking ownership of their information. Unless and until this extra effort is recognized by the leadership of the unit as a valid use of time, it will not happen. Unless and until the specific value of the information a unit produces is established, there is no chance to get support for the extra effort.

There is a Catch-22 here. To get value, the unit has to create good information. To create good information, however, the unit has to see the value. This is where many units stand. You can break this deadlock by making a strong yet simple argument for an investment now against future returns on a unit's information.

Allow Information Source Ownership

In the long run, you can establish in some groups complete ownership for the information they produce. In these cases, the unit maintains its own repository of the information types it owns. It owns the information model for its information and distributes it to others in the organization for use in various outside systems and publications.

For example, suppose you are in the investment analysis group of a financial services firm. Your group holds the organization's brain trust on all issues related to investment. Your analysts are primarily concerned with figuring out what investments to recommend. They work directly and indirectly with customers to help them manage their portfolios. Given the typical state of information, this group will not put much effort into producing generally useful information. What it does produce will be inconsistent and idiosyncratic.

Analysts might even hoard information and consider it their personal source of advantage over other, less informed colleagues.

But let's suppose this group is different. The group decided that it can make much more progress as a group by taking the information seriously. The group is tired of its customers not getting good information through the systems that IT has provided, so it has taken matters into its own hands. The group is also smart or experienced enough to do what it needs to do to own the information.

The group begins by taking back ownership from the IT group. Instead of authoring into five different systems, it authors into one system, its own. The system then produces output for the various IT systems that need to use the information. The group has information types called Investment Tips, Fund Advice, Investment Product Backgrounders, and many others. The group has also spent considerable time studying the consumers of each type of information they produce. The structure and rhetoric of each item for each type are designed to make the relationships between analysts and customers smoother and more productive. And it has worked. Since the group took control of investment information, its two most important progress indicators—customer satisfaction and number of transactions per month—have both risen.

Now suppose your strategy contains the following Strategy Statement:

> *If we deliver Investment Tips to small investors, they will invest more of their available funds.*

You determine that posting tips on the Web is a good initial way to deliver them to small investors. So you contact the analyst group to get access to their information. They agree with your Strategy Statement, but their own analysis shows that the Web is not the best way to deliver tips. They feel that an email channel with the tips linked to backgrounders on the Web would be better. However, they agree to work with you. They already have a Tip information type that is being used in training materials and telephone scripts. It will take some work to define which tips should be given to small investors, but they agree to undertake this work because they can use the same categorization scheme later when they attempt to convince you to invest in a batch email system. You work out an agreement with the analyst group that calls on them to supply tips at a certain rate and in a certain form. Everybody is happy, and within a few weeks of the first conversation, tips are flowing to small investors.

Wouldn't it be nice if units could be partners of this sort in information management? If they were this serious about their information, your job would be seriously simplified. Of course, most units are nowhere near this serious or well organized. They are too new to the information management game to even know they should be this organized. But maybe there is at least one unit in your organization that could be this serious, if you provided the leadership and training to get them there.

I describe the idea of authors and sources more fully in the ebook Leading Information Departments at www.laughingatthecio.com.

Part 4

Lead Across

Decide which groups are the most important suppliers to the most important audiences with the most important information. As opposed to the groups that you have worked with most or those that are most eager to work with you, these are the groups you should be working with.

Information management may be done today in some strange ways.
Beginning with the most important groups, enter and then drive
the information management conversation.

Approach these groups proactively, beginning at the top to establish the right rapport and rules of engagement. Make sure you have a very good idea of what you want from the group and what you have of equal value to give them. Plan your approach rather than letting it evolve over the course of chance meetings. Understand that the groups you approach have their own, often arcane ways of managing information. Respect these ways, but be clear that in the future these old ways will not suffice. Take the best of the older

117

attitudes and methods and coalesce them into a new way of working that frees information from both a print and Web mentality. Avoid the traps of thinking that managing more information is better and that centralized systems are better than distributed ones. Effect the most impact by managing the least information in the least central way.

Chapters in This Part:

Chapter 11: Engage Intelligently – Be smart about how you roll information management out to the organization. Reach out to important groups with a well-articulated value proposition. Identify key players and court them. Educate and advocate wherever you go.

Chapter 12: Move Management Forward – People who have traditionally been in charge of important information have not always made the transition to new channels. People who were never supposed to be professional information suppliers are now called upon to be just that. Your job is to ease everyone's transition to a new world of management and publication.

Chapter 13: Do Less – Just because someday all information will be electronic does not mean that you need to control all information centrally now. Quite the contrary, most information is not worth your time. Centralize storage when it makes sense, not as a matter of course. Control information only if you can't manage it. Never own information if you can help it.

Chapter 11

Engage Intelligently

Be smart about how you roll information management out to the organization. Reach out to important groups with a well-articulated value proposition. Identify key players and court them. Educate and advocate wherever you go.

Just because IT is a service organization does not mean that it needs to be a reactive organization. On the contrary, if you believe in the "Radar O'Reilly" school of service (see the Conclusion, Be the Information Guys, at the end of the book for more information), you'll agree that to serve you have

Don't let projects become power struggles.
Create rules of engagement that work for all players.

to be extremely proactive. Why then do so many IT groups wait until organizational units approach them to initiate any projects?

Walls have been constructed between many IT groups and those they serve. In addition, most IT groups would not know what sorts of projects to propose to their client units. The clients themselves often don't know what projects are most important. If you understand the nature of the deadlock between IT and its clients, you can help break it down. If you have a strategy, you will know what projects units should be doing even if they don't. Finally, if you think clearly and carefully about the people that client units comprise, you will see how to approach them and engage them intelligently.

Break the IT Deadlock

There is frequently a confrontational or adversarial relationship between the IT group and the other parts of the organization. This amazes me—not because it is hard to understand but precisely because it is so easy to understand! Most people already understand the basis of this conflict and still no one seems able to do anything about it. Table 11.1 dramatizes the typical terms of the conflict and suggests reasonable compromises between the warring parties.

Table 11.1 IT in Conflict and Compromise

Other Group	IT Group	Compromise
We just want to get something done. That IT group puts insurmountable barriers up against getting anything done.	We are inundated by ill-conceived proposals of questionable value. We need some process to assure that what we are asked to do is feasible and a valuable use of our time.	We don't create process for process's sake. We will demonstrate the business value of any process we employ. We understand that you do not have the experience to formulate a proposal that is specific enough for us to accomplish. So we will help you.
They only do the projects they want to do.	We only do the projects that we are able to do.	We do the most important projects as defined by our validated and published strategy.
The whole point of an IT group is for them to help me figure out how to use technology. Instead, they treat me like an idiot while they speak geek to me.	People do not understand the consequences of what they ask for. They don't want to learn either. They just want us to say we'll do it and not ask them to understand anything.	When we are defining a project, we speak an information management "Lingua Franca" that is easy to understand and focuses entirely on business value. During implementation, as our problems get more specific and technical, we will still present alternatives in the common tongue, but we will expect that you will make an effort to understand technical trade-offs in the terms by which we define them.

They are really strict. They won't let anything we do go on any official computers.	We have been burned many times by flaky software that crashes and brings everything down with it. Then, who gets blamed for downtime? Us!	There are levels of reliability and support that we offer. At a minimum, we can house your software on an isolated computer and allow you to run it. At the maximum, we can certify the reliability and safety of your system and run it on our enterprise critical computers.
We are forced to create our own systems, and then we are forced to support them indefinitely because the IT group can't or won't.	They come to us with all this bizarre stuff and expect that we will figure it out for them when their guy quits or they run out of money. They never ask us to help until there is a crisis.	We are really good at figuring out bizarre systems and helping you get them in order. We are also really good at determining what systems are valuable enough to the enterprise to justify that sort of effort.
They just don't get it. We talk about business goals, and they talk about bits and bytes.	They just don't get it. We talk about analysis, requirements, and architecture, and they don't know how to answer.	Let's start by talking about what you need to have happen to advance the goals of your group. Then we'll help you work through to a solution that will get you there. We'll try to understand the attributes of your business, if you will try to understand the attributes of the software process.
They don't get the Web. They think it is just another technology.	We are not artists or writers; we are technologists. We make the server work. What to put on the server is their problem.	We can't and don't understand the details of your information. We do, however, understand very well how to help you collect your information and distribute it on the Web and wherever else it needs to go to work for the organization.
They want to own everything and won't let us even get to our own information.	Whatever we don't control is a risk. There is no end to the ways they can corrupt the data and bring down our servers.	You own the information and as much of the infrastructure for managing that infrastructure as is feasible. We will teach you how to own it. We may have to charge you for fixing it if you break it, though, but we'll be fair.

In summary, the IT group feels cornered, constantly blamed for failures they were never consulted about, and pestered to support other people's messes. The opposing group just wants some help, and all they get are guarded gates and techno-babble. The key to breaking this deadlock is to redefine the terms of the discussion between IT and the groups it serves. The IT group needs to climb out of a strictly technical perspective, and the other groups need to understand that computer systems are critical but fragile. IT staffers are scared and for good reason. They have been burned by systems that fail or mire them in endless changes.

Both groups need a process and a shared vocabulary with which to craft, monitor, and amend agreements. As you might expect, I believe that language could be the language of information management that I present in this book.

What goals are you trying to serve? Who is critical for meeting those goals? What is the minimum amount of information you can deliver to make tangible progress against those goals? These are terms that everyone can understand. An agreement on goals, audiences, and information is a tangible agreement on what a system will deliver. It speaks directly to the basic goals of the client unit and it can directly drive systems analysis and design for the IT group. Further agreement on more specific information management entities can further nail down the relationship using terms that both sides can understand.

I provide details about the information management entities in the ebook Leading Information Strategy at www.laughingatthecio.com. The most detail is in Content Management Bible at www.cmbible.com.

If a system delivers the agreed-upon information to the agreed-upon audiences in the way it is supposed to, then all is well. If along the way, it becomes difficult to meet this specification, then the system specification can be renegotiated. In the heat of a project, however, it is not always feasible to conduct such abstract discussions. The project should always be guided by your goals, information, and audiences, but sometimes you still have to dive into the details of either the information system or the business processes that it supports. In those cases, you just have to make the effort that is required to understand the other's world. But in most conversations, especially at the start of the project, you can use the information management terms I have presented to craft solid specific agreements that are actionable within the IT group and deliver clearly defined value to client groups.

Proactively Approach Groups

In the short term, adopting a Lingua Franca and meeting other groups halfway will get you on the road to happy, mutually beneficial relationships. In the long run, you have to engender a sense of the seriousness of information in those same groups. A serious attitude will lead to serious gains against business goals.

Rather than waiting for groups to approach you, approach them. Analyze their situations and figure out how and when to go to them with proposals. The switch from reactive to proactive is easy to make if you take the right approach. The right approach begins, as usual, with your strategy.

Your strategy should tell you which groups are the most central to supplying the most important audiences with the most important information. These groups—as opposed to the groups that you have worked with the most or those that are most eager to work with you—are the ones you should be working with now. Once you've identified the top groups, you can map

> **Q** Can you help us build x (a portal, content management system, intranet, etc.)?
>
> **A** Why? What will it do for us? In particular, what information will it deliver to whom? And having gotten that information, how will those people be better off? Then what will they do for us so that giving them information was worth the effort? Oh, you don't know all that. Well, let's chat again when you do.

the qualities that enhance or inhibit your ability to work with them. Some of these qualities are:

- **Their relationship to the strategy** – You will need to go to the group with a specific vision of what they could be doing. Detail explicitly what goals, audiences, and information the group impacts. Consider how much they are likely to agree with your assessment and decide which parts of your strategy you would be willing to modify if they are unwilling to play.

- **Their leadership** – You will need solid support from leadership. Who is in charge of the group? Do you have an existing relationship with them? Who controls both groups? Are they encouraging or hostile to the idea of information management? Do they or could they understand the idea of information strategy? How much direct support and involvement can you expect from them?

- **Their information management staff** – You will need this group to either do some of the work or support your staff's work. In any case, you don't want them to undermine your work. What sort of editorial, development, infrastructure, information architecture, and design staff does the group have? Are they working with any outside resources?

- **Their perceived and actual audiences** – You will need the group to take your audience definitions to heart and orient to them. Do they have a current notion of audiences? If so, how does it match with yours? How serious are they about studying and serving audiences? Have they established a priority order for serving audiences? How does it compare to yours?

- **Their attitude** – You will want to instill a positive attitude toward the hard tasks of information management. How do these people view information management (if at all)? How do they view your group? Have there been problems in the past? Do they get the basic value proposition of information management? If not, where are the barriers? Who are the opinion leaders in the group who you might need to work with?

- **Their pain** – Your proposed systems must address the known problems in the group. If you know what disappointments and defeats the group has suffered at the hands of unwieldy information, you are in a better position to propose a solution that speaks to their heart. Has the group tried information management in the past? With what results? Are they being crushed by loads of information? Is site maintenance a huge burden or cost? Have they failed to get contributors to contribute? Knowing their pain, you can be sure to address it.

- **Their process** – You will need the group to adopt some fairly strict processes. How process-oriented are they now? Do they have and enforce rules of information production? How amenable would they be to increasing the seriousness with which they create information? Are there camps of high-value information providers who cannot be controlled or who are deeply committed to the way they do things now?

- **Their tools** – You will want to use or supersede the technology the group now uses. What authoring or tagging tools are in use? Do they use any content, asset, document, or other management systems? If so, how are they working? Do they maintain their own infrastructure? Are they happy with their technology platform, or are they ready for a change?

- **Their current channels** – You will need to use, extend, or supersede the communication channels the group currently employs. How does the group communicate now with its audiences? How do these channels compare with the ones your strategy specifies? Do they understand and can they master the channels you propose they use? As of today, how well suited is their information to being delivered through your proposed channels?

I provide details about the idea of channels in the ebook Leading Information Departments at www.laughingatthecio.com.

If you do your homework on the groups you need to engage, you will have more than enough material to develop plans on approaching them.

Even if you don't get an exhaustive view, you will no doubt be able to answer the question:

Is this group a net asset or liability to our strategy?

Even if it is just a gut feeling (or maybe especially if it is a gut feeling), if you believe that this group will take more effort than they will return in value to the organization, approach them slowly or not at all. If this group was added to your list of important units, you probably can't avoid them forever, but you may want to see if you can't put off official contact until you have had a chance to ameliorate some of the bigger issues. Because these bigger issues are almost always about people and their attitudes, fixing the problem might be difficult. The most potent salve I have found for soothing bad feelings with one unit is to be popular with the others. After a string of successes, units that once looked down upon you can change their minds and come courting. Likewise, if you stop pursuing a group in favor of other more suitable part-ners, jealousy might also soften their attitude. The card I least like playing is to go over their heads. It's often easy to appeal to the group leader about her staff or to the executive above the leader about her. If you do this, of course, you risk the enmity of the person you "ratted on."

In most cases, the situation is not so dire that you need to avoid an important group but not so rosy that you need not even plan the approach. Use the simple principles described in the following sections to form an engagement plan and put your relationship with important units on the best footing possible.

Form a Value Proposition

Put yourself in the shoes of the group you want to engage. The group is not looking for extra work; it is probably a bit scared of the information because it has some indication of the magnitude of the effort required to organize it. The group may also be wary of working with your group because of past fail-ures on your part or theirs. You can expect at least a few hurdles to overcome. So, ask yourself:

Why should they play? What is so compelling about helping the organization manage information that they should start devoting themselves to it?

Be prepared to dislike the answer you come up with. The sad fact is that the equation does not naturally balance for many groups in your organization. The benefits of information management do not always accrue to the suppliers of information (see the "Take Information Seriously" section in Chapter 10, Devolve Ownership, for more on this idea). Be honest with yourself about the trade-offs for the groups you need to work with. Craft the sweetest deal you can and begin thinking about how to sweeten it still. If you end up in the enviable position where the group stands to gain much more from information management than it will cost, then be ready to ask them for more support. Of course, the group itself probably does not have a solid sense of the value of information management, so you might have to figure out the value of their info and then tell them. Compare your ideas to their native notions of what is worthwhile to do and to convince them that your analysis is better. It may be a lot of work to convince the group that it stands to gain by managing its information. What's worse, convincing them it is important is just the precursor to the real work of getting the group to help you do the job.

Form a Key Person Plan

Identify the particular people in the group with whom you need to establish good working relationships. Understand current attitudes, figure out who should be responsible for cultivating the relationship, and decide what exactly the person could do for you. There is nothing manipulative or Machiavellian about this; feel comfortable telling key people that they are key, and why. This will help your relationship more than not telling them. Key people come in these varieties:

- **The group leader** is key and so might be some of her lieutenants. You might want to take responsibility for these relationships yourself.

- **Project and team managers** might be key. Your corresponding managers can take care of this group.

- **Information management practitioners** within the group may be key, especially if they are opinion leaders or recognized experts.

- **Content contributors** are always key. Without their support, the best laid systems grind to a halt. Find the contributors who set the pace for the rest and those who are early adopters. If you are lucky, the same person might serve both roles.

- **Content holders, information gatekeepers, and administrators** are almost always key. These people often manually do the work of an automated information management system. They are administrative assistants, researchers, librarians, archivists, editors, and even interns.

They know what information is most important, and they know how people look for it. Find these folks and court them. If they feel that your system will replace them, there will be no end to their passive resistance. If you show them that they can use your system to raise their visibility or position in their groups, they will be your staunchest allies.

Your success with every group depends on how the group accepts you. If you have done your strategy well, you will have a convincing rational argument for working with you. If you have done your key person plan well, you will have developed empathetic ties to the people in the group that can make or break your rational plans.

Form an Education Plan

As you know, information management is new. Most of the approaches I propose are new, and they are sometimes very different from the way things happen now. Resistance to these new and strange ways lessens quickly as needs are understood and benefits increase. The groups that are the most eager to embrace information management are those that have figured out what the heck it is and how it is a way out of their perceived pain. If you can figure out who needs to know about information management and get them to know it, you will have removed most or all of the barriers to adoption.

Chart Engagement Tactics

Before you make proactive contact with a group, you have the opportunity to find out a lot about them. You can study their readiness for information management, craft a value proposition, identify key players, and chart an education plan to fill any knowledge gaps. Even with all this under your belt, it is still worthwhile to approach groups in a premeditated and organized way. Here is one way to premeditate your engagement.

You Approach First

You should approach the leaders of the group first. This establishes your relationship with the leaders and allows you to craft a workable and mutually beneficial agreement up front. The agreement ought to be first and foremost based on your strategy (or on negotiated changes to it). You and the leaders can then use your agreement to resolve issues escalated to you later by the project team. I strongly recommend explicitly documenting the agreement you reach. Make it official and pass it out to both teams as the starting place for all their work. Wave it at people who try to drag your work off-track.

The official agreement is one thing; the interpersonal agreement is another. Base interpersonal agreement on the value proposition you have crafted. Give leaders a chance to negotiate amendments to the proposition and work it over and over with them until they are confident that the work you need them to do is worth it. The value proposition is the basis of your working relationship with the other group. The other group should be clear how they are helping themselves by helping you. You can count on leaders to use the same arguments you make now to lobby the rest of their group on your behalf.

If your approach to the other group ends in an agreement, you will have accomplished a lot. You will have the official definition of what your work together will accomplish for the organization. Most importantly, you will have established the trust and respect of the group leaders. The official agreements you reach are only as good as the good faith of the people who crafted them. If and when times get tough, it will be that good faith, not the words of your agreement, that will pull you through.

When a deal is struck, you have the opportunity to go the next big step with your colleagues. Share the rest of your analysis, key person, and education plan with the leaders. Enlist their help in correcting, refining, and finally owning the plans. Make joint plans for how to approach the rest of the group. Bring in some key people and enlist their early support as well. Your aim here is to prepare the way for your team and show that you have carefully thought through the initial issues of the engagement. Help the leaders and key people figure out how to angle the value proposition to appeal to diverse factions within their group. Get them to take on some of the task of educating and recruiting key people. Establish escalation paths from both teams to their leaders. Figure out when you will need to talk again and how you will jointly arbitrate disputes. In short, forge a high-level alliance.

Throughout this process, keep this thought in mind:

> *This time, you have come to them with a viable strategic project. You have done the information strategy work for the unit you approached. Whether they know it, you are training them for the future when they will do this work by themselves. Consider what you can do even now to make that day come sooner.*

At this point, if they are not thoroughly impressed with the thought and effort you have spent on them, they were definitely not worthy of that effort.

Have Your Team Approach

If your initial contacts with the group went as they should, you will have given your team a gift they will surely appreciate—strong terms of engagement, good faith, and a clear escalation process for their issues. You have put yourself in a position of authority, not control. You will have embedded your success metrics (progress against your strategy) firmly in any projects that emerge but without restricting the specifics of how they are met. Not bad for a short analysis and a couple of meetings with people you should know anyway!

Your team can follow you into the engagement confident that they are set up for success. Here is the order in which your team might now enter the engagement:

1. **Your business analysts** can engage next to fill in the details of the deal. They can use the framework I provide or their own process to establish exactly how the work with this group will result in advances to the goals of the organization.

2. **Your other analysts** can engage next to determine the specifications of the systems that will create, acquire, tag, store, manipulate, retrieve, transform, and deliver the information people need to help you reach the selected goals.

3. **Your technologists** can engage last to determine the software and hardware needed to implement the specification that the analysts have crafted.

You can find out more about these jobs in Content Management Bible at www.cmbible.com.

I don't intend this to be a strict order or for you to exclude anyone who I put in the process later. But clearly, I believe that you should not, as most IT groups do, lead with the technologists. I also intend to establish an orderly transition of responsibility from the people with the widest view of the problem to those with the narrowest view. However, feedback in the other direction is critical to assure that the people at the higher levels (and you, in particular) stay in contact with the implications of what they propose. If you follow the checkpoint process that I have defined, you will remain in contact. (See the ebook Leading Information Departments at www.laughingatthecio.com). If you encourage your analysts and the leaders of the client groups to do the same, they too can get constructive, actionable feedback.

Move Management Forward

*People who have traditionally been in charge of important
information have not always made the transition to new
channels. People who were never supposed to be professional
information suppliers are now called upon to be just that.
Your job is to ease everyone's transition to a new world
of management and publication.*

I am of two minds concerning information management. On the one hand
I truly believe that the change afoot is as great or greater than that caused by

Use every lever at your disposal to advance the cause of
information management. But be patient; it will be a long transition.

the invention of the printing press. On the other hand, I believe that there is nothing new here. All organizations have always used information to present themselves, and some organizations have always distributed information as their product. And just as the printing press revolutionized the distribution of information without changing the kinds of information that people wanted to distribute, the new electronic media have changed the means of distribution again without changing the information distributed.

If there is nothing new here, then why have so many organizations faltered in their adoption of electronic information systems? Those who have traditionally been in charge of important information have not always made the transition to the new channels we have created. Just as scribes did not always become printers, printers have not all become digital distributors.

Transcend the Print Mentality

Many, perhaps most, publishers, authors, and editors in your organization have not made the transition to digital publication either because they don't want to or because they don't know how. I'll never forget the conversation I had with the CIO of a large publishing company whose product is information. After a long and very productive talk about the promise of transcending the company's print mentality to find a new way of producing and distributing information, the CIO told me that he agreed that electronic information was the future and that he ought to be doing something about it. Then he told me that he wouldn't do anything about it because his staff would rebel and many would leave.

"They are QuarkXpress people," he told me, "and they won't stand for using any other tools."

QuarkXpress is one of the applications commonly used to create printed publications. What this man told me, in effect, was that his staff would rather quit than change its publishing tool. The staff had invested many years mastering one application and felt that they should be spared having to learn any others.

This group clearly did not want to change. They saw themselves as printers not information providers. Printers print. They use tools and processes that result in paper and ink landing in a reader's hands. Information providers provide information. They don't care how the information is delivered as long as consumers get the information they want via the channel they prefer. They surely choose their channels carefully, but the channel is subservient to the result of a successfully met information need.

I have no problem with printers or even those who prefer QuarkXpress. For that matter I have no problem with people who define themselves as Web site creators, animators, video producers, or mobile phone screen designers. They have valuable skills that should be cultivated. I do have a problem when any of these people feel that they can own the information that they distribute and create it in such a way that others cannot easily use it.

We've been talking about print publication groups, but the problem is everywhere. Throughout the organization, people live with the comfortable but untenable assumption that the information they produce is for a single purpose and that they can create it however they want. This attitude stops many worthy information initiatives in their tracks. When information providers simply refuse to produce information in a usable and reusable way, information stops flowing.

The people and groups who refuse to change will eventually grow old and move out of the organization; they will be replaced by younger people who have no stake in the earlier methods and are comfortable moving on to new software applications the way their parents moved from records to tapes and then to CDs. Until then, reluctant contributors are the most significant opposition you have to information management. They often resist passively but effectively.

From my all-too-easy perspective outside this organization, I was tempted to tell my CIO client that he was better off without his recalcitrant staff. But I did not. I understood that, contrary to what his staff might think, they are not powerless and what they will and won't do really matters.

There is no categorical answer for what to do with staff who will not change. On the other hand, there are good answers for what you can do for staff who will not change. In my experience, most people would change the way they create information if they could just figure out how. In fact, I have seen what seemed to be a steadfast resistance to change quickly whither in the face of a lucid, well-articulated vision of a new process and its benefits. This vision, when followed up by a step-by-step migration plan, removes much of the fear that people secretly harbor.

Therein lies the rub: If you cannot articulate a vision for change or if the vision does not persuade people that their efforts to change will be doubly rewarded, then it is not fear but prudence that prevents people from changing.

I detail some specific approaches for dealing with the print mentality in the the ebook Leading Information Departments at www.laughingatthecio.com.

It's pioneer days in the era of information management, but I believe that history will be on our side. If we really are in the information age, then eventually treating information with care and respect will become the norm. If you are not up to the challenge, you too will eventually leave or be pushed out of the lead position. But why not take the challenge? Why not relax into a career-long, career-making experiment in freeing information from the constraints that people mistakenly put on it?

Transcend the Web Mentality

Information management is not about the Web. It is about all available channels of communication. The Web was simply the force that pushed most organizations beyond a single channel. With the Web, a second very important channel was opened, triggering a wave of new thinking about information delivery. Unfortunately, that new thinking was wrong much of the time.

When the Web "hit," a new generation of heavily caffeinated and very enthusiastic practitioners took over, not because they had mastered information or communication, but because they had mastered the new technology. To them, the Web was the beginning and end of information delivery. They confused, exactly as the QuarkXpress people had, the medium with the message. Many (though clearly not all) became "Web people." The Web was the channel. All other forms of publication would be subsumed.

That, of course, has not happened. More material is printed and read offline today than ever before. But the Web people missed an even more important point. As "information people" clearly recognize, content can and should be separated from presentation.

When there is only one channel of publication, it is hard to tell where the channel ends and the information begins. If you only have a Web site, then information and HTML seem to be the same thing. But as soon as you have two channels, you can either deny the legitimacy of one of the channels (as both Web and Print people have often done), or you can recognize that the information is different from the way it is presented and consumed. Information is not Quark or HTML.

Print people usually resist passively, fighting what they mostly perceive as a rear-guard action. Web people, on the other hand, often fight righteously and fiercely to win the entire world over to their view. They have the naive optimism and self-confidence of a young nation only recently discovering its power. Even while many of the techniques they think they have invented were, in fact, reinventions, they have the zeal of true believers, and it is sometimes hard to resist their enthusiasm. However, as the number of important channels increases (handheld devices seem to be the next wave), it becomes harder and harder to justify locking information into a single channel. And just as you need to transcend the limited and older print mentality, you also need to transcend the seemingly forward-looking but just as limited Web mentality.

Respect the Wisdom of Traditional Publishers

In the old days of print publication (a scant 10 years ago), tried-and-true methods and job roles assured a quality product. Writers, editors, designers, illustrators, and printers worked together in a tightly knit group to produce publications that were useful to the organization. The publications department was responsible for publications. Its world was stable if inglorious. The tools used, even when first computerized (a scant 20 years ago), were designed for experts. Training was assumed. The format and structure of the publications produced was also stable. Printed materials have been around long enough that their production is a thoroughly conventional process. Not so for electronic publications.

Print: Permanent or Temporary?

Once upon a time, the printed document was the real one, but not any more. It used to be that hard copy was "ground truth." It could be trusted because you could touch it and it couldn't change once it was in your hands. Now we look at the printed version with suspicion, sure that the "real" one has been updated and that our paper copy is invalid. We print things out for the convenience of reading and out of habits that feel quainter each year. Our metal file cabinets, once the source of reference for all words, are now filled with words that we never refer to because the "real" one is in an electronic file on our network. Even our archives, where the definitive version of a document once resided in a cardboard box, are now on disks and tapes in a data warehouse. Even the word "document" has changed allegiance. Now a document is on a computer, while a printout is on paper.

It is a profound role-reversal that has happened so smoothly that no one has really noticed. Paper is now a temporary and disposable storage medium, while bits and bytes are the permanent and authoritative media.

When the lifespan of paper documents is only hours or days, how long will it be before we have printers that recycle paper and ink directly? The old paper goes in the back, and the new paper comes out the front.

It has always seemed strange to me that the old publishers did not immediately see the promise and pitfalls of electronic publications. They did not, as I would have expected, seize the new forms. They didn't take ownership of the Web and begin an organized generalization from the old tools, jobs, and products to ones that could embrace all forms of publication. Instead, many buried their heads and ignored the new channels that spread far and wide before them. They left it to others to own the new channels. With the rise of easy-to-build Web sites, anyone could become a publisher, and many did. Most of those who rushed in had no background in "classical" publishing. And since the trained publishers were often absent, they were left to create or fail to create their own practices. Their declaration that they were inventing the future was not questioned by the people who should have known that they were just repackaging the past.

The wisdom of the few publishers who did pursue electronic information was overwhelmed by the naiveté of the swarms of new people coming into the field. Plus, the sheer volume of information that organizations wanted to publish precluded a more prudent approach.

Information is not so much undervalued as underdeveloped in most organizations. If you can somehow imbue your Web and other electronic publishing processes with the traditional wisdom of the industry, you will be way ahead of the pack. Look around your organization. Find some of the old hands who have grown up in the old world of structured publication process. If they are not too print-prejudiced (or cynical), bring them into the mainstream of your new information management initiatives. Try balancing the exuberance of the Web people with the seasoning of the more tenured publishing staff.

Create Authors

The new field of electronic publishing was not dominated by publishers. It was also not dominated by professional authors. Authorship, once reserved for people who made a profession out of it, has expanded to include anyone who has anything to say to anyone. Before the Internet, an author was someone who wrote for a living. After the Internet, an author became anyone who can type and has knowledge that their organization wants them to share. Today, the large majority of information that is published on the Web is created by people who have another job. Even if they wanted to care about the information they produce, they would not know where to start. Moreover, few organizations teach information-creation skills or reprimand or reward staff for the information they produce.

In future generations, our definition of literacy will expand to include authoring for electronic distribution. Today, our employees remain largely illiterate in these matters. Whether you like it or not, if you want to do information management, you will have to train your staff to author information and train your managers to value the creation of information.

There is more about author training in Content Management Bible at www.cmbible.com.

Use Editors

In the print world, editors have always been at the center of activity in the production of information. I have been disappointed to see them move consistently rearward in the electronic world. Editors have always served two basic functions: to make information stylistically and mechanically consistent (usage, punctuation, format, grammar, and so on) and to assure that the information makes sense and communicates well (good arguments, right tone, responsive to the audience, and so on).

These jobs are no less important today than they have ever been. However, because of the influx of nonprofessional authors, more lax publishing standards, and the enormous volume of information most organizations handle, editorial process has become an expensive luxury. We have more information from more people now, but it is inarguably of lower quality.

To be fair, editors, used to their tried-and-true methods, have done little to make themselves more relevant. In particular, they have not risen to the challenge of extending editorial workflow to include tagging and metadata standards as well as language standards. A few years ago, I coined the word metator to cover this new job. (For more information, see Content Management Bible at www.cmbible.com).

Just as editors make information linguistically consistent and ensure high quality, metators make its metadata consistent and ensure high quality. The mindset is the same (good command of language and an eye for detail), and the methodologies are the same (editors create editorial process and metators create metatorial process), but new people have come in to fill the jobs. To be sure, many editors have made the transition, but many more have not. And those who have become active in metadata and workflow are not the leaders they could be. Blame surely lies with the editors themselves for not bringing their skills into the present era. But blame lies too with their editorial managers and ultimately with IT leaders who have not understood how to use their editor's skills.

Once again, the people we most need to do information management are not the ones who are doing it. Bring editors, or at least editorial process, back into the flow of information from creator to consumer. Identify editors in your organization who are capable of leading metadata and workflow, and then get them into these positions.

Be Librarians

Librarians have felt the pinch of organizing information bases for as long as libraries have existed. Librarians organize and provide access to large volumes of information. Whether they oversee books, periodicals, images, sounds, or moving pictures, librarians create and maintain collections, catalogs, and content. The parallels to the concepts of information management should be obvious. Just as a library does, your systems maintain collections, catalogs, and content.

How does a librarian know where to look for the information you need? How does a librarian even know what you are talking about when you say what you need? A trained reference librarian is somehow able to pull from you a usable definition of what you want and then can figure out the best way to find it. The process of finding out what you want is generally called a reference interview. It consists of asking a set of questions that narrow your possibly vague initial request into a set of phrases that can be used to search a specific set of information sources. Again, the connection is clear. If you take a lesson from the reference librarian, you will not assume that users know the words to use or know where to look for the information they need. You may even discover that hiring a reference librarian to help people navigate the trickier parts of your information is the best way to ensure that people find what they need.

Librarians invented and commonly use the hierarchies, indexes, and cross references that provide access to information. Each library's collection is organized into a taxonomy that's no more than a hierarchy. Librarians use all kinds of indexes to map the keywords of a collection to each other and to the content in the collection. Cross-reference strategies lead the visitor from one category of book to the next. The reference librarian is also expert at turning a vague question into a firm strategy for access. In both their conceptual categorization of information and very practical strategies for finding the right content, librarians hold the keys to finding what you need to organize information and make it accessible.

Finally, librarians embody the soul of the information management discipline. At the core of librarianship is the idea of service and intellectual integrity, unfettered access to information and the honest desire to arrange knowledge so that everyone can use it. What better philosophy could there be upon which to found your own information management group?

Not all librarians understand the central and vaunted position that they hold in the information management landscape. Others understand but prefer "the smell of the stacks." Still fewer information leaders understand the potential resource librarians and librarianship represents to their organizations. Now that you have read this, you no longer have the excuse of ignorance. If your organization has librarians, bring them into the fold. If you don't have librarians, get some.

Chapter 13

Do Less

Just because someday all information will be electronic does not mean that you need to control all information centrally now. Quite the contrary, most information is not worth your time. Centralize storage when it makes sense, not as a matter of course. Control information only if you can't manage it. Never own information if you can help it.

Your goal is not totalitarianism.
Don't centralize and rule over information.

The most fundamental question that your group must answer is, "Why are we here?" I think you can guess my answer to this question. You are here to make sure information does as much for your organization as it possibly can. It's that simple, or at least that simple to say.

I devote most of this book (and others as well) to describing how you can make that happen. In this chapter, I would like to discuss instead some answers to this question that are neither simple nor, in my view, correct.

Don't Just Centralize Information

I'm not sure how it happened. Within a few years of the advent of the Web, people realized that someday all information would be electronic. Somehow this perception morphed into the idea that organizations need to house and distribute all information from a single central repository as soon as possible. From there, the central repository became the main, and often the only, aim of information management. The reasoning goes something like this: Our information today is a mess. No one can find what he or she wants, and sharing information is impossible. We have all these information silos that prevent us from getting full value from our information. We need to get information all in one place, interrelate it all (using enterprise taxonomies) and allow anyone to get at and reuse any piece of information they want.

The idea sounds great in principle, but it will never work. And even if it could work, it would not necessarily result in more value coming from your information because:

- It supposes that you have the time to gather and relate all the information in your organization. You don't. Even if you could figure out in theory how to relate all information, you would never have the time to gather and look at it all. A lot of information is created and changed spontaneously. You could never keep up with the flow.

- It supposes that you can figure out how the organization's information is related. You can't; there are just too many ways that one item of information could be related to another. Without some serious and artificial limitations, you'll lose your mind trying to anticipate all the associations.

But suppose you could somehow figure out how to relate all information, and suppose you could muster the effort needed to gather and tag it all. Why would you want to? The ideal, often tacitly accepted, is that anyone could get to any piece and reuse it in any way. But what percent of the information that is centrally housed would ever be accessed, let alone reused? Only the tiniest fraction.

Let's just take one type of information as an example (in an entire organization, there are many, many more). Suppose your team carefully files every piece of correspondence received in case anyone wants to see it again (it has been tried). Each time they receive an email, a letter, a phone call, or a text message, you might have them fill out a computerized form that identifies the correspondence and how it relates to the other correspondence they and others have received. What would happen if you tried this?

First, you will have a heck of a time designing the forms for people to fill out. What should you say about each piece of correspondence so that other people could reliably find it? But suppose you could figure out the forms; your next hurdle would be to get the team to fill them out. If it takes one minute per message and there are 100 messages per day, people will spend almost 25 percent of their day cataloging messages! But suppose that, despite the problems, you did get them to spend this time. How often will someone find a piece of correspondence that he or she needs using the system you have created? Even when he or she takes the effort to look (which won't be often), he or she frequently won't find what they are looking for because of the amount of information stored in the repository and how richly connected it is. Engineers call this a low signal-to-noise ratio. I call it Google!

Even if you could magically get some system to automatically store and catalog your emails (there are a range of products on the market that claim to do this), you would still have to deal with a haystack of junk for every needle of useful information someone might find.

Multiply the experiment above by the hundreds of information types your organization handles, and you will clearly see the absurdity of the idea of a comprehensive enterprise repository. The fact to face is that you have resources to tag, store, and deal with search results from only the smallest fraction of the information you hold. Luckily, you don't need to tag and store everything because only a small fraction of your information carries the majority of the value. The problem is to separate the valuable stuff from the much larger mass of less important stuff.

Most people have never thought through the ramifications of a single central repository; if they had, they would not talk about it. People love to take a great idea and extend it to absurdity. The great idea is that the information you need should be easily accessible when you need it. The absurdity is that *all* information should be easily accessible in case you need it. Sadly, the absurd idea often stands in for the great idea when the information leadership does not know how to separate the information wheat from the chaff.

Manage the Least Amount of Information

The belief that more information is better is part of the strange machismo of the information management field. When we evaluate Web search engines we ask first, "How many pages does it index?" When we talk about our sites, we start by noting how many pages we have. We think that the point of information management is to capture and manage more and more. In fact, the point of information management is to manage the least amount of information that will help the organization achieve its goals. Management is expensive and most information is not worth the cost. Add to this already damning argument the truth that the more information a system holds, the less likely you are to find the piece that you want (signal-to-noise ratio again), and you have all the justification you need for aggressively restricting the information you manage. This is not to say that the vast unwashed mass of information should not be produced, however; it is to say that you should care about as little of that information as possible.

When I do a search on Google, I'm impressed with the number of results I see. But impressed quickly turns to being depressed when I think about reviewing them all. What I would really like on Google—and what it seems to me you would be better served to aim for in your systems—is to do a search and return only one result—the right one.

Many teams set their sights on delivering any needed information to anyone who might need it. Your team would do better to aim to deliver the least possible information to the smallest group of people who can tangibly help forward the goals of your organization. Don't worry though; even the smallest amount of the most essential information is still likely to be more than you can handle.

Don't Control Information; Manage It

Just as the idea that we are here to manage all information has crept into the souls of many IT groups, the idea that we are here to control information runs deep as well. The argument goes something like this:

> *If we don't exert control over our information, it will be a mess. Without a firm hand on the creation and structure of information, everyone will do it differently and we will not be able to share it.*

To this seemingly reasonable argument, I say, "Yes ... but." Yes, people will not be consistent in the ways they structure information; yes, it is hard to share information that is not consistently structured. But, by enforcing standards, the following happens:

- You may end up driving the value of the information down. For example, suppose you decide that any sort of narrative document you manage will be called a white paper. You create and impose a structure based on the white papers you have studied. Along comes a group with information that is more like a story than a white paper, but you make them create white papers because that is what you already have. If the group is relatively powerless, they will buckle and do it your way. With more power or chutzpah, they will fight you or go around you. Either way, the information loses.

- You may end up stopping the flow of information. Every structure rule and metadata field you put in front of a contributor raises the barrier to contribution a bit higher. Make the barrier too high and people won't get over it.

I don't like the idea of controlling information because it goes against the idea of service and value. But I do like the idea of managing information. Management implies a lighter touch. It also helps you to be less idealistic and more practical in your approach to information.

A practical, managerial approach to information structuring might entail the following:

- Create the least amount of structure necessary for the job. Each rule of creation (templates, styles, allowed parts, and so on) and each metadata field has to have a specific justification for specifically foreseen uses (see the "Destroy the Myth of Future Returns and General Solutions" section in Chapter 14, Set the Tone of the Department, for more on foreseen and unforeseen uses).

- When in doubt, include less structure, not more.

- Calculate the structure load you are putting on your various contributors and make specific plans for how that load will be met.

- Be prepared for the structure of your information to change over time. Start your structure simply, and plan for greater complexity over time.

Be humble in your approach to structuring. Your team should keep an eye on the more comprehensive and structured future of your information but remain solidly anchored in the messy present. They should not restrict contributors too much now for the sake of dubious future information-sharing needs.

Own the Management, Not the Information

After many aborted attempts to get people to participate in Web systems, one information management group was told this by their executive:

> *Your job should be to create and deliver all the information that people need.*

In addition to their usual jobs of delivering information, the group was expected by this executive to originate, or at least find and take control of, whatever information anyone needed. The idea was absurd on every level:

- While well connected, the group (a whopping six people) had little or no subject matter expertise.

- Other people throughout the organization were already creating information and were not interested in turning it over to a third party.

- The team's skills were in Web development, not authoring.

- The plan was completely unscalable. As the team took ownership of more and more information, there was no provision for them to hire more and more staff.

Needless to say, the plan did not go very far, but the intention was honest. In the face of trying to get other business units to cooperate, the executive just gave up.

Your group should not own information; it should own management. Business units should own information and your group should help them. Within business units, the people who best know the subject matter and the audiences should own information. There should be as direct a link as possible between information creators and consumers. While easy to describe, this level of "ownership devolution" is hard to achieve. In fact, you may be a long way from creators who are savvy and engaged enough to be good owners. Still, at every opportunity you should push originating groups to own what they produce while you support them with training, standard tools, workflow processes, and information structures. With this kind of support, originating groups have little excuse for not doing their part.

There is more on this subject in the ebook Leading Information Departments at www.laughingatthecio.com.

Balance Central and Peripheral Resources

In most organizations, the struggle between centralizing and distributing is perennial. It's not just an IT problem; it's a human problem. Societies, clubs, families, and every other group of two or more people go around and around with this issue. In the IT world, it usually takes the form of the following question:

Should we have a corporate IT group that controls all technology spending, or should we distribute IT budgets across business units?

As in all enduring dilemmas, no one knows the answer (or it wouldn't endure). My approach to such dichotomies is to declare them false and move on. Do we really have to choose? Can't we have a central unit and distributed budgets? Can we get the best of both worlds? Better minds than mine have tried this approach, and the dilemma remains. Still, I think there are some points of clarity in this otherwise confused dialogue:

- It matters less whether you are centralized and more how well all players follow the same strategy. As the terrorist group al-Qaeda and all guerilla groups before them have shown, you do not need direct commands to be coordinated, but you do need to be coordinated to have an impact.

- If you are too dispersed, good people might not come and stay in your organization. Good people want established career paths. If a great information architect is recruited into a decentralized IT group, will she be able to continue to advance within her profession or will she hit a ceiling?

- If you are too centralized, your staff will have a harder time keeping close to the subject matter and business units served. You may want to put an IT team within a business unit or make your teams go "on-site." Either way, teams who are remote from the people they are meant to serve don't do well.

- If you are too dispersed, your staff might not maintain discipline awareness. If your designers are spread across the company in ones and twos, they may not be able to leverage each other's knowledge. Of course, just because you pack them all into a central unit does not mean they will work together, but proximity helps to create a critical mass of information sharing and mentoring.

- If you are too central, you may stifle creativity and autonomy in approach and technology. Central groups can easily lose touch with the evolving problems and homegrown solutions that people constantly come up with "in the field."

- If you are too dispersed, you might inhibit information sharing. Groups who are not in contact have little reason to coordinate their efforts.

Whether or not you centralize staff, you should make sure that infrastructure, processes, information structures, and technologies are central enough to guide and facilitate the work of distributed groups. For example, a single solution/tool to templated authoring in Microsoft Word can be developed centrally and used by teams throughout the organization.

So what's an information leader to do? A little of both, I suspect. You might try differentiating central IT from peripheral IT by promoting the attitude that central IT is bigger, more serious, and more for the large, unit-spanning projects, while peripheral IT is more creative, faster moving, and capable of solving more department level problems. While both central and peripheral IT justify projects on the basis of the strategy, on the periphery, the strategy is interpreted more to meet local needs, while at the center, projects with significant impact on primary goals are done more often. Central can vet and promote standards and best practices (most of which might come from the periphery). Let a thousand ideas bloom on the periphery and make sure the best and brightest are promoted and refined at the center.

People might move to this sort of periphery if they want a bit more action and creativity; they might move to the center for career advancement and increase in the visibility of the work they do.

However, you can balance the centripetal and centrifugal IT forces, keep a strong sense of law, order, and justice in mind. The law and order are derived from your strategy. The strategy keeps the field level for all staff regardless of where they are in the organization or what they do. If they are advancing the strategy, they are doing well. Justice can only come from you. If you set a strong example of applying the rules fairly and judging people and projects on clearly articulated and well-documented standards, your staff will do the same.

Part 5

Lead Down

Many supposed information leaders are actually irrelevant to their staff. This is unacceptable. Luckily, it is also easily remedied. You can adopt a fairly simple design philosophy, project process, and review policy that will keep you ahead of your team without interfering with them.

Organize and transform your group's ad-hoc and possibly chaotic approach to information.

Develop a standard approach to ongoing projects and new project proposals that sets clear criteria for what sorts of projects get support and that involves you only at the critical times in the project process.

Chapters in This Part:

Chapter 14: Set the Tone of the Department – Before launching a new approach to information management in your group, make sure there is no residual ill will from the past. Don't let projects be derailed or unduly influenced by specialists with the loudest voice or greatest numbers. Recognize there is a wide variety of perspectives from which information systems should be designed. Finally, combat the natural tendencies of your technologists to create elegant systems that provide lousy information.

Chapter 15: Build an Information Practice – Build an organization that naturally translates enterprise strategy into action. Establish the foundational practices that help you take that action. Create a department strategy that implements enterprise strategy. Create a constantly updated palette of departmental tactics that implement department strategy. Make sure your staff grows into the department you are creating and that you balance consistency with creativity.

Chapter 16: Lead Information Projects – Establish excellence in information management as a central tenet of your group. Establish yourself as the holder of the enterprise strategy and the final source on how that strategy applies to projects. You do not need to be involved in every aspect of your projects to make sure they are high yield.

Chapter 14

Set the Tone of the Department

Before launching a new approach to information management in your group, make sure there is no residual ill will from the past. Don't let projects be derailed or unduly influenced by specialists with the loudest voice or greatest numbers. Recognize there is a wide variety of perspectives from which information systems should be designed. Finally, combat the natural tendencies of your technologists to create elegant systems that provide lousy information.

Clearly establish a new regime in which professions
do not vie for position.

A new attitude and way of doing business will not just occur in your department. In fact, it may be years before your group fully embraces a new way of working. Some will leave if they feel you are taking them in the wrong direction, or at least away from where they want to go. Others, however, will be attracted to your vision of the way your department works, and slowly the tide will turn.

Your IT group should look to you for perspective, wisdom, and overall direction. You can provide all of this and more if you try. But before you can become the sage for your group, you will have to clear away any debris that may have accumulated over time, either because of the leaders that preceded you or because of your previous style. Here are some of the comments I have heard that illustrate the divide between professionals and their leaders:

- "He is clueless. He has no idea what we are doing. It's embarrassing to even talk to him about it."

- "She thinks she knows what we do better than we do. On the basis of no evidence or experience, she tells us in micro-detail what to do. When her ideas flounder, she is not around to pick up the pieces. Better to avoid her."

- "We have no relationship or rapport. I only ever get directives from him. I can never get on his schedule."

- "She doesn't know any more than me. When I have asked advice in the past, it has not helped, or it has been obviously wrong. I'm afraid to ask for advice because it might be wrong, and I will have to follow it anyway."

- "He is always busy at the higher levels of the organization. I'm not a priority, so I don't expect consideration."

- "He yanks us around too much. He provides new directives at every meeting. He never remembers the old ones that he made us change direction to work on. It's too jarring to the team to include him."

These criticisms boil down to "She's interfering," and bubble up to "He is irrelevant to our work." In either case, the project team avoids the executive because he or she has nothing of value to offer them. If they felt that the executive understood them, brought new information to the table, and would not thwart their current efforts, they would surely come for help.

So how do you stake out this position between micromanagement and no management at all? The answer comes from what IT groups generally lack and why they often fail:

They don't know how to judge the value of the systems they create.

You can fill this gap by having a clear idea of value in your own head and by holding your teams to that idea before and during their projects.

Don't Default Leadership to the Professionals

IT groups often end up dominated by one professional faction or another. In addition to technologists and business analysts, IT groups generally contain writers, editors, information architects, project and production managers, producers, designers, analysts of various sorts, and a variety of media (video, sound, animation, and so on) specialists. Each of these groups of people has its own perspective on the sorts of projects they prefer. If one subgroup is dominant, the IT group as a whole will do the sort of projects the dominant group prefers. If no one perspective dominates, the group will bicker incessantly as each type of professional vies for control over the creative direction of the group. When, as often happens, there is a person from one of the disciplines who is capable of taking a wider, more strategic perspective, she is often given lip service with no real support from the others. Without an outside voice to unite all the perspectives toward a common enterprise-level goal, the group stands little chance of seeing a bigger picture.

I don't mean to overstate my case. I know a number of IT groups that do try to think strategically and do succeed to some extent. In these cases, a leader has emerged (one who is often not the appointed leader). The leader does her best to understand what information the organization most needs to do its job and then tries to get the team to do it. But the best natural leader in the world is only guessing if she does not have the active participation of those in the organization who know what the business goals are and how each business unit can forward them.

Someone in the organization needs to lead even the best teams. Without this outside person keeping the team's eye on the real prize, at best the group will stumble toward strategic systems, but more commonly, they will just stumble.

So how can you prevent your teams from stumbling? It isn't difficult, and it needn't take much time. Helping the team certainly does not mean becoming one of them, as many executives seem to think (see "Lead, Don't Practice" in Chapter 16, Lead Information Projects). Executives mistakenly suppose that because they don't speak Geek, Designese, or ArchitectTalk, they have nothing to say to the team. I've seen many executives lapse into a hypnotic head nod when barraged by the lingo of the teams they lead.

When a team comes to a meeting and begins unloading its specific, lingo-bound problems on an unhappy executive, it is a sure sign that the teams needs the executive's input—not to solve the particular problems but to rephrase the questions. A team that does not rise above its internal concerns to meet the executive on her own terms is doomed. Because the team can't express thoughts in the language of the executive, the team is left to use its own language to communicate. The smart executive recognizes a "teachable moment" when she sees one and cuts the techno-babble short. She drags the team out of its comfort zone and into the realm of strategic thinking.

Of course, to drag the team into strategic thinking about information management, the executive must have done some of this strategic thinking beforehand, or she must at least know what it means to think strategically about information. Then she must formulate that thinking into strong, clear questions that challenge the team to step out of its daily concerns and consider what exact value the system it is considering can bring to the organization.

Design from Multiple Angles

Discussion in your team will naturally center on designing and building information systems. As a foundation behind all such discussions, you should have a persuasive opinion about the attitude your team takes toward system design. You should let your team set the standards on a technical and even architectural level. But it is uniquely your responsibility to set the tone of the group on the higher levels. In this section, I'll present a number of different design perspectives that you can adopt or reject and blend as needed to set the tone for your group. As you'll see, each perspective puts a different stakeholder at the center of the system.

Design for Users

Most good software development teams follow a user-centered design philosophy. In essence, this perspective states:

> *A good system gives its users an easy-to-use way to get the information they want.*

The system designers understand their audiences well enough to ensure that the information the system delivers is relevant to the needs of each audience. It is also designed for ease of use. The audience understand the words it uses, is familiar with the controls it employs, and can navigate the system to find answers.

You probably have some user-centered pros on your team (if not, you should). You are also likely to have some user-centered zealots. Once at the fringes of software development, the user-centered perspective is now at its center. It is used as a prime justification, a guiding perspective, and the basis of the process for every part of the software (and Web) development lifecycle.

User-centered design is a good thing. It makes systems accessible to people without a technical background, decreases learning time and increases productivity. Your teams should fight to use it. You, however, should understand that user-centered design is not the only design game in town. You should be willing and able to balance the user perspective with other perspectives that also need to be accounted for and incorporated into your systems.

Design for Experts

User-centered design has in recent years triumphed over what should have been (but never was) named "expert-centered" design. In this, the original paradigm of software development, the program's creator (there were no Web sites back then) poured his (there were few women back then) understanding of some problem space (finance or manufacturing, for example) into computer code. Operators (they were not called users back then) would type arcane programming-like statements after a blinking prompt on an otherwise blank screen. Good or expensive systems would come with extensive documentation that described in horrifying detail all the permutations of all the commands that were permitted. Operators were expected to study the documentation for a long time before typing their first command.

Can you guess why this could have been named expert-centric? To do a task, the poor user had to almost become the expert. Today, of course, user-centered design reigns, and the expert has to almost become the user before the first line of code is written.

However out of favor, the expert-centered perspective has its place. For one thing, if you have a highly technical audience that prefers a command line to a Graphical User Interface (GUI), then user-centered design becomes expert-centered design. More importantly, the expert-centered design embodies this critical idea:

> *A good system tells its users what they should do even if that makes it harder for them to use the system.*

The idea is that people who designed this system are smarter than the user. It is worth the user's time to learn the words the experts have used and the controls they have concocted. It is not sufficient to simply give people what they want, because they don't always know what they need to accomplish their task. You sometimes have to teach them about the problem and then teach them how to use the system to overcome the problem.

This perspective is, in a way, the opposite of user-centering. However, there is no need to make your systems choose. Your systems can be user-centered, reiterating the user's expectations, and expert-centered, taking users beyond their expectations to new ways of understanding a problem. But this is tough, especially in the current backlash era when user-centering is well on its way to becoming dogma in the IT world.

Design for the Organization

This book is primarily about organization-centered design. The organization-centered attitude is defined as:

> *A good system gives the organization what it wants at a reasonable price.*

My entire strategy process is based on this simple proposition. It is the attitude I have suggested you take in deciding on projects, and it builds upon my ideas on how you can lead throughout the organization. Unfortunately, it is a perspective that can easily get lost in projects if it is not continually reiterated. Why? Because it is in the self-interest of the team-mentors to put their perspectives instead in the middle.

In the user-centering revolution, someone finally stood up for the rights of the great disenfranchised user community. Experts too had their day. So where are the stakeholders who represent the organization and why aren't they standing up for their right to be in the middle of design? The organization pays the bills. Systems are supposed to be created specifically for the benefit of the organization. So what's going on? If you haven't already, these are questions you should start asking of yourself. Could it be that the IT leadership of the organization has not stood up for the rights of the organization?

Design for Technology

Technology-centered design says:

> *A good system uses the best technology.*

This attitude is true as far as it goes, but it often goes overboard in one of two ways. The first and more understandable way is driven by techies. As you should expect, people who have built their careers on technology derive a certain part of their identity from the technology they own. At parties with other geeks, they talk about the latest versions of the coolest applications. They compare CPU speeds, bandwidth, and drive sizes. It matters to them viscerally and professionally how far behind the leading edge they are. So there is no mystery why they prefer projects based on technology. And because the same type of person excels at rattling off scary warnings and sophisticated justifications in words that nobody else understands, it is no wonder that they are often taken too seriously.

The other way this attitude goes overboard is more pernicious and harder to understand. It is the bad attitude of executives. This attitude often takes the form of empty edicts that spawn big go-nowhere projects. When the Web first emerged, many executives decided that they needed Web sites long before they decided why. As each new technology buzz hits the world stage, executives seem to need one of those as well. From Knowledge Management to CRM to ECM and RFID, there is always a compelling justification and a lot of hype in the trade press. Naive executives flock to new technologies. They know they need that new thing even if they don't know why.

The dot-com bust cramped the style of these people. Technology for technology's sake went seriously out of fashion. However, no amount of downturn will change the basic "gear head" or "insecure executive" personality. There will always be people pushing for projects simply because they implement the next great technological silver bullet.

Is there no good and proper use of the techno-centric attitude? It is becoming increasingly popular now to rally around the cry, "It's not about technology." I have certainly done my part to raise the call. But is it never about the technology? Let's not throw the baby out with the bath water. New technologies are like new powers that are suddenly at your disposal. You would be ill advised not to take a hard look at each one and decide what problems it solves. It is only when the solution precedes the problem, when the technology is adopted before you know why, that technology-driven design goes too far.

Design for Everyone Else

For brevity, I won't detail the many other perspectives that might drive design. Instead, I'll just list a few for you:

- **Team-centered design**, which claims that a good system saves the information management team time, money, or stress. Your team would not be a good team if they were not always coming up with new ways to do their work better. You would not be a good boss if you could not tell the frivolous from the worthy ideas.

- **Contributor-centered design**, which claims that a good system saves the people who create information time, money, or stress. Especially in situations where you have reluctant or naive contributors, this is an important perspective.

- **Publication-centered design**, which claims that a good system produces the best output. Web projects especially have placed a high premium on the quality of the output (sometimes to the point of handcrafting every page). However, whether it is Web sites, handheld screens, emails, print materials, or all of the above, many people and especially the art and design staff feel that this is the best place to ground all the rest of the project activities. You would do well to recognize and temper this attitude with the others I have described.

- **Information-centered design**, which claims that a good system best represents an information base. Precious few people would go so far as to claim this as the central driver for a project, but it is nonetheless a perspective to use in cases where the information is particularly valuable to your organization.

There are constituencies for each of these design perspectives. An ideal project balances all of them, simultaneously optimizing each perspective to give maximum benefit to all stakeholders. But when was last time you ran an ideal project? In real life, there are constant struggles to pull a project in one direction or another. Teams dominated by one constituency or another will pull projects toward one center or another. Sometimes an important perspective is not represented at all, and the project fails because of it. More often, enough of an attempt is made to satisfy the most salient perspectives to make sure the project does not fail, but it is far from optimum.

It is your job to make sure each perspective is at least considered. When you find a perspective that has not been taken into account, bring it up, and ask the team why it is missing. If you want to be an activist leader, begin to figure out for yourself what the right mix of perspectives is for a particular project and lobby for it. In any case, make sure your staff can adequately represent each perspective and that there is a balance of power that prevents the overt domination of a perspective to the detriment of your efforts as a whole.

Destroy the Myth of Future Returns and General Solutions

There is a pernicious attitude in IT groups that turns small, focused projects into big unwieldy ones without regard for the organizational returns. It comes from the core philosophy of technologists and causes them to advocate passionately for efforts other than those that return proven value. The attitude is:

Behind every particular problem is a more general one. If we solve the general problem, the particular one will be solved as well. If we solve the general problem well, we will have a usable solution to an entire class of problems.

This is an attitude upon most technologists (programmers in particular) were raised. For example, good code is general code that can do the following:

- Be used for a wide variety of problems

- Be called generically by any other program that can supply a few guiding parameters to it

- Detect and handle exceptional situations

- Fail gracefully under exceptional situations that it cannot handle

- Have an intuitive and robust user interface

- Scale to larger and larger problems

- Run as quickly and efficiently as possible

It is a good attitude in many cases. Unfortunately, in the messy, ambiguous, exception-fraught, and ever-changing world of information tools and applications, good code is hard, even sometimes impossible, to create and often not worth the cost.

Don't build a tool just because your team says it will always be able to use it. If the tool is not justified on the basis of real savings to real work that is going on now, beware. More often than not, future returns do not materialize. If I was an investor and a tool was a stock, I would give no more than 15 cents on the dollar for the savings you say you will get someday for a tool you want me to pay for today.

Seasoned programmers know this, though they may be reluctant to admit it because it means that they get to do fewer fun projects. Things change. What you need a tool to do later often requires it to be substantially rebuilt or discarded entirely.

At any rate, future returns are by no means guaranteed by vague statements like "We will always need to …" or "This problem comes up over and over" or any justification that includes the word "cool." The way to deal with future returns is to quantify them exactly the way that you quantify current gains. Ask what specific known or reasonably predictable uses are there for this tool over the next year? In these uses, exactly what time-savings can the tool be reasonably expected to return? I would still discount these predictions by half, but if they sound reasonable, then the additional returns can be added to the value of the tool.

Generality is a slippery slope that has landed me on my butt more times than I care to admit. All programmers want to create code that is useful for a class of problems not just a single problem. On the other hand, generality, as with future returns, is hard to take to the bank.

For example, consider a Web page dissection tool that is meant to automatically open a particular set of 10,000 old Web pages and convert them into database records. The tool programmer will be naturally pulled to develop not just a tool that can dissect the particular 10,000 pages she knows about but any Web page. She will look for the general principles of HTML to find the ways that her code can detect any possible structure to slice and dice a Web page however needed. Only after trying for a long time to do this, she may realize that such a general solution is hard to come by. First, it may not exist. In many information management problems, there is no general solution even though it seems as though there should be. At first glance, you might be tempted to say that there must be a way to automatically dissect any HTML page. But in practice, there are so many ways to mess up HTML that you will be unlikely to find, let alone know what to do with, all of them. This is not just an HTML problem. In fact, HTML is relatively well behaved. Most other text environments are even less parsible and less amenable to general-purpose solutions. A good programmer will respond here that she can indeed create a general tool if you just give her time to do it.

And, of course, that is just the issue. Whether a general solution to the problem exists or not, the real question is how much effort you should put into looking for it. The slippery slope of generalization tends to be exponential as the chart in Figure 14.1 shows.

The more general your solution, the more effort it takes, the harder it will be for people to use, the more it will cost to get them to use it, and the more likely it will crash. You need to find the point of quickly diminishing returns.

Future returns and general solutions are often used to justify each other. The reason we need a general solution is to get future returns, and the future returns are why we need a general solution. Use the same critical approach: Exactly how much generality is needed to meet the needs of projects we know we have or can reasonably expect to have in the next year? How much effort will it be to generalize rather than stay specific? Balance the return with the effort.

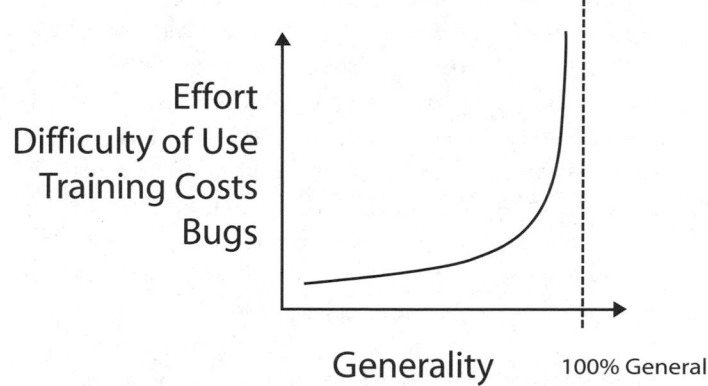

Figure 14.1   Be sure to stay on the friendly part of the curve!

Love, Hate, and Computer Systems

The relationship between people and their applications can be almost as complex as their relationship with other people (especially if their personal relationships are a bit impoverished). Take Ernile, for example, a fictitious but not implausible character.

His life was tough before that first system came along. There was no joy in his work and he felt like quitting. He pinned a lot of hopes on the new system and expected a lot from it. In his first couple of interactions with it, it seemed great. It would meet all his needs and make his life much happier. But the honeymoon was soon over. True, the system did save him work, but not nearly as much as he had hoped. It was cranky and hard to deal with. It had a million little quirks that he had to work around. It didn't make nearly the impression on other people that he had hoped it would, and it sometimes embarrassed him by flipping out in front of strangers. After a few months, he wanted to just dump it and get a new one.

But over time, he developed a strange appreciation for the system as well. There were definitely cool and fun things he could do now that he could never do before. He learned its interface inside and out, and he made sure it would perform well in public. Its features were really well-constructed, and its logic was quite deep. He found himself feeling protective of his system when other people would criticize it, and he would work hard to defend it and to make sure that it always performed as well as possible. Still, many times it made him so frustrated that he wanted to kill it. But he always calmed down and found a way to go forward with it.

Other people were far less understanding and wanted him to dump the system as soon as possible.

They would say, "You can do way better, Emile. You are smart and resourceful. You don't have to put up with all the grief that system is giving you."

Emile was conflicted. Sometimes he would nod in an uncommitted way; other times he would get offended and reply "What makes you think any other system would be much better? They all have quirks. Better the devil you know ..."

In the end, he dumped the system; times had changed, and he could no longer hold on to it. After that, he went through a series of systems. They were all quirky, and none of them fulfilled all his goals. His current system is really pretty good. It rarely lets him down and has a beautiful interface. But to this day, when he is working late nights, he still thinks about that first system and how intimate he had been with all its features. He wonders, "Could I have made it work?"

It is natural for programmers to want to find a general solution. A less natural attitude, but one for which you should reward your programmers (and other staff), is that there are no final solutions or ultimate tools. There are tools that are worth the effort and there tools that are not. This change in attitude may well be the largest and hardest change you will make. It strikes at the heart of what technologists pride themselves on: robust, general solutions to difficult problems. Behind this pride is the assumption that there is a solution to the problem, and if you are good enough, you will find it. In scientific, accounting, and manufacturing applications, this attitude might work. But in information systems, there is not always a solution. Information is messy, inconsistent, and extremely hard to pin down. Clearly there is a lot we can do to automate its collection and distribution. But just as clearly, there is a point of diminishing returns after which automation is not worth the effort.

Destroy the Myth of Full Automation

Technologists prefer general solutions. They also prefer fully automated solutions that require no human intervention. Teach them to put their desire to remove people from the process in the proper perspective. The proper perspective is that full automation is a nice idea but is wrong to pursue single-mindedly because:

- It often can't be accomplished. Information is ambiguous. As often as not, it needs the interpretative power of a well-trained human mind to figure out what to do with it.

- It is often not desirable. Information that is too standardized, too regular, and too predictable (in other words, able to be automated) is boring. People may not want to consume it, and it will fail at its rhetorical purpose (see "Information Persuades" in Chapter 6: Know Why Information Matters).

Instead of establishing full automation as the goal for your group, establish the idea that:

> *The best system maximizes a person's impact on information. It removes repetitive time-consuming activities and focuses the person's attention on the tasks that require their intelligence and interpretive power.*

The automation system helps people; it does not replace them. The system design recognizes that people cannot and should not be removed from the process. Instead, people are designed into the system at places where a dumb computer could never handle all the nuance, creativity, humor, passion, and persuasive power that good information should have.

There is more about this idea and an example in the ebook Leading Information Departments at www.laughingatthecio.com.

Of course, people are a limited and expensive resource, and having them in the middle of every information process would be impossibly costly. Luckily, if you have established a good strategy, you have a basis to decide which information is worth the cost. You have the basis for working around the limitations of full automation, and you have a basis for reigning in the attitude that values full automation over full information.

Chapter 15

Build an Information Practice

Build an organization that naturally translates enterprise strategy into action. Establish the foundational practices that help you take that action. Create a department strategy that implements enterprise strategy. Create a constantly updated palette of departmental tactics that implement department strategy. Make sure your staff grows into the department you are creating and that you balance consistency with creativity.

Span information management and information systems in your group.

Your chief goal as information leader (CIO, director, what have you) of an information department (IT, IS, ICT, what have you) is to build a coherent perspective and methodology for the strategic management of information. If you have developed an enterprise information strategy (see Chapter 9, Create an Enterprise Strategy), then the mission of your department is easy to state:

> *Our department helps the organization collect and deliver information to audiences to maximize progress against the goals of the enterprise.*

It's easy to state but not so easy to do. But if you work carefully through the implications of this simple statement, and keep the end in mind of building systems that support the strategy, then a clear idea of an "information practice" should emerge. In this practice, information professionals craft information tactics to make incremental progress against your department and enterprise information strategy.

Set Department Strategy

The strategy of your department states how you will deliver on the wider enterprise strategy; how you will amass and distribute a well-defined base of information to a well-defined set of audiences to meet the goals laid out in the enterprise strategy. While your department's tactics change frequently, your department strategy should evolve slowly. The pyramid shape of strategy and tactics are shown in Figure 15.1:

- **An enterprise information strategy** works at the level of the entire enterprise. It states how you believe information can best serve the goals of your organization. (You can learn more about enterprise strategy in the ebook Leading Information Strategy at www.laughingatthecio.com).

- **A departmental information strategy** works at the level of your entire group (the IT department, for example). It states broadly how you will collect and distribute information.

- **Departmental tactics** work at the level of particular projects and systems. They implement your information strategy by stating the specific measures you will take to turn your strategy into projects, processes, and systems.

Your enterprise strategy sets the standards to which all your department activities must respond. And while the basic goals, audiences, and information should be set at the enterprise level, your department still has to operationalize the strategy as follows:

Figure 15.1 Department tactics are the foundation for a department strategy, which is the foundation for an enterprise strategy.

- **Goal Rationalization** – The enterprise strategy states what the highest priority goals are, but it is up to your group to figure out how to turn the goals into something that can be measured and used as a guide for determining the methods that most impact the goals.

- **Audience Division and Profiling** – The strategy tells you who the most important people are, but your department must figure out how to put each information consumer into the right audience and what data you will maintain for each person. Most importantly, your department will have to decide how to relate audiences to the specific information they need.

- **Information Structuring** – The strategy names information types, but there is a long way to go from a name to a usable information model. Your team has to decide how to model your information types and how to share that model with all contributing groups and individuals.

I cover these subjects in detail in the ebook Leading Information Departments at www.laughingatthecio.com.

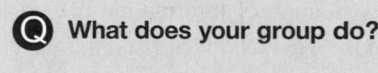 **What does your group do?**

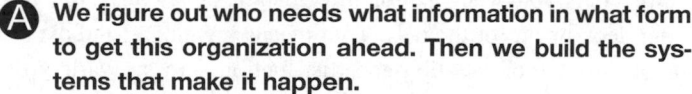 **We figure out who needs what information in what form to get this organization ahead. Then we build the systems that make it happen.**

Briefly, an operationalized enterprise strategy becomes a departmental strategy when you begin to consider how to best originate, manage, and distribute the information:

- **Originating Information** – Given the range of information types and audiences you will have to cover, what is the best way to understand, organize, and serve the authors of the information? What existing sources are there for the information, and how should you engage with them? The answers to these questions and others form the basis of a comprehensive origination strategy (getting valuable information in a way you can use it).

- **Managing Information** – How will you store and retrieve information? Will you have one database or many? How will you organize and share information with contributors and distribution outlets? The answers to these questions and others form the basis of a management strategy (making information as structured and available as possible).

- **Distributing Information** – What channels (Web, printed materials, broadcast, email, and so on) do your audiences use? What publications within each channel (Web sites, brochures, podcasts, and so on) will best communicate the information? The answers to these questions and others form the basis of a comprehensive distribution strategy (getting the right information in the right way to the right people).

The "classic" IT vision is to use technology to advance the goals of the organization. That vision has not changed under this new regime. The primary difference between this vision and the "classic" is that origination, information, channels, and publications are between technology and goals. If you did no more this quarter than establish this vocabulary as the recognized way of talking about your work, then you will have taken a giant step toward making information work in your organization.

Continually Craft Tactics

The jump from print to electronic distribution of information has created enormous opportunities for an organization to get its information to important people. However, if you want to use information effectively, you have to organize your department for the task. That means organizing and overseeing the process of information creation and distribution across a variety of creators, consumers, and delivery platforms. It can get complex fast. Without a well-thought out and rigorous department strategy, you will not be able to take advantage of the opportunities. Without a leader pushing the development of these capabilities, they may not develop.

Your department's tactics are those activities that implement your strategy. While the tactics should change frequently, the strategy should remain stable. Even though the tactics you employ will change, the basic types of tactics available are constant (see Table 15.1).

There is more information on all these subjects from a leader's perspective in the ebook Leading Information Departments at www.laughingatthecio. com. The most detailed practitioner view on these subjects can be found in Content Management Bible at www.cmbible.com.

In summary, establish a set of tactics to support your department strategy for collecting and distributing information. Using the terms I have presented here (and your own modifications), you can build a comprehensive and shared understanding in your group about what your tactics are and how you should manage them. Of course, what you say will in part determine who can (and who wants to) talk with you. Expect that if you change the terms of discussion in your group (and beyond), you will attract new people and repel those who have nothing to say in the new language.

Cultivate Key Skills

To do information management, your group will need to be good at a number of specific technologies, tools, and concepts. More importantly, however, you will want to cultivate key skills that underlie information management:

Rationalizing information, people, and process. Database people will be familiar with this term from the many times they have had to rationalize data. When you rationalize information, you take the inconsistent and contradictory information you are presented with and turn it into an ordered, well-defined, and sensible (rational) form.

For example, when you say that your organization has 23 types of very important information, you are not identifying distinctions that already exist so much as you are attempting to impose a workable order on the tangled mess of what already exists. The beauty of a good rationalization (in information management as in psychology) is that it quickly becomes reality for those who buy into it. Your teams need constantly to rationalize the undifferentiated mass of people, processes, and information into a model that is easily understood and accepted. Still, while rationalizations are made, not discovered, some are closer to the truth than others. Make sure yours prove themselves over time to be accurate, workable descriptions of your information environment.

Table 15.1 Information Tactics

Tactic	Description	Example
Projects and Initiatives	Short and longer-term endeavors that yield a particular gain against your strategy within a given schedule and budget. Initiatives are long-term movements to improve an aspect of the flow of information from the organization to its audiences. Projects deliver a particular result in a particular time frame.	You might create a long-term initiative to develop your communication with small customers. Within that broader initiative you might create a project to deliver "Advice" and "Resource" information items via text message to small customers.
Systems	The applications and processes that facilitate the large scale movement of information from origination to audience. They are the hardware and software needed to gather, store, and deliver information.	You might decide to create or buy a content management system to collect, manage, and publish "Advice," "Resource," and other information types.
Tools	Smaller applications that facilitate one or a few aspects of the movement of information.	You might decide that you can harvest "Advice" items from emails with text parsing and analysis scripts.
Workflows	The processes you develop to organize and scale the movement of information.	You might decide that "Advice" items (as well as a number of other information types) should go through a specific lifecycle (creation, review, distribution, re-checking, and retirement, for example).
Channels	The ways information flows from your organization to its audiences.	To deliver "Advice," you might need to develop advanced capabilities in text messaging.
Publications	The specific containers of information that package it in a way that one or more audiences want.	You might create a publication called "The Advisor," targeted to small customers and delivered through the Web, print, and text message channels.
Access Structures	The ways you categorize information so that you can manage it and your audiences can find it.	You might need to develop a product taxonomy to categorize your "Advice" and other information types so your customers can subscribe to the ones they want.

Modeling. A model is a version of reality that focuses only on those attributes of reality that are important to your purpose. For example, suppose you decide to store only a name, an age, and a household income for each person that you deliver information to. From these few facts, you can decide into what audience a person fits and what information to give them. Obviously, there is quite a bit more to a person, but the model can safely ignore it. You modeled your audiences from the vastness of what it means to be a person, and found you could get away with capturing only three small bits of data. It's a nice, simple model of a very complex reality. Yet it allows you to get your job done. And that is the basic goal of all modeling: to reduce the complexity of your subject as far as you possibly can without compromising your ability to get your job done.

Operationalizing. Making your understanding of people, processes, and information actionable is perhaps the hardest but most important of the skills you need. It is one thing to understand your audiences; it is quite another to turn that understanding into a profile that can drive information to all audiences through all channels. For example, when you operationalize your understanding of the review process, you turn it into a named set of steps that let you assign responsibility, monitor progress, and chart blockages and bottlenecks. You make the process actionable by your organization and amenable to automation.

Your team has to be good at rationalizing the infinitely complex world of people and information into a simple model of that world that operationalizes abstract concepts into ones that you can assign, monitor, and hopefully automate. Luckily, these skills are already in today's technology departments. In fact, they are much better understood by technologists than by other information professionals. However, while technologists often have a knack for reducing complexity to a manageable level, they are prone to throwing the baby out with the bath water in the process. Models in the information world need to be far more complex, flexible, and extensible than those in the data world. And, while it needs to be rigorous, an information model also needs to allow the creative and persuasive nuance that good information demands. Furthermore, instead of ignoring (or denying) the nuance of information, you have to model what it means for a particular type of information to be persuasive or even creative. If you can do this, you will have started to integrate the simplicity of modeling with the infinite complexity of people and information.

Your team had better get used to evolving their models to deal with continually changing conditions. You may find that you have competitors with rationalizations that are different than yours, that your models are too simple or, just as likely, too complex, and that you will be asked to do more and more operationalization as time goes on. Right from the start, take the attitude that your team is there to make and remake sense continually. Each time the sense changes, they change their models to follow suit. Embed that fluid attitude into the foundation of your department structure, and you will avoid a lot of frustration.

Create a Repeatable Process

Information originates in a fundamentally creative and usually individual act. It begins when human beings with something important to say have the skill and determination to say it well. The management of information, on the other hand, is a pretty mechanical task. It can require highly trained and intelligent people, but at its base, information management is like a factory. Good information arrives at the factory in raw form. The factory's machines, which are run by trained technicians, strip, segment, convert, and tag the raw information to turn it into items that can be automatically stored, retrieved, packaged in publications, and delivered through channels.

The information leader does not have to work on the factory floor; she doesn't even have to design the factory process and machinery, but she does have to fully appreciate what it takes to build and maintain that factory. Ideally, she could design the information management process if she chose to do so. But at the minimum, she makes sure that someone designs and runs an efficient and effective process, that the process is not blocked in any way by the wider organization and, most importantly, that the factory is producing goods that are worth more than the cost of production.

A well-thought out and rigorous information-management process encompasses and integrates the needs, abilities, and attitudes of contributors, consumers, staff, technology, and information. It promotes the creative process needed to originate information, but it is overlaid with a set of templates and guidelines that enhance consistency and reduce the amount of effort needed on the information factory floor.

The factory nature of information management is covered in detail in Content Management Bible at www.cmbible.com.

Chapter 16

Lead Information Projects

*Establish excellence in information management as a central
tenet of your group. Establish yourself as the holder of the
enterprise strategy and the final source on how that strategy
applies to projects. You do not need to be involved in every
aspect of your projects to make sure they are high yield.*

IT groups traditionally excel at building systems that satisfy constraints.
Give them a set of well-conceived (and unchanging) requirements, and they
will give you a dynamite system. They have not done as well at identifying
constraints, however. The system requirements IT groups collect are often
spotty and at the wrong level. This leaves large gaps that must be filled in by

Map out an appropriate project process and then assure that
project territory is equitably distributed among the professionals.

the intuition of the developers. They can be too broad and not give actionable direction, or they can be too specific and constrain the technical solution too much.

IT groups have also not done well at all at deciding which systems are worth building in the first place. To create projects, they rely on simple executive directives (like "We need a portal") or requests from business units (like "Our site is out of control"). Given a set of projects, it is often difficult for IT groups to prioritize them. Typically, the projects with the loudest or most important sponsors get the most attention. Many IT departments never originate a project idea and think of themselves only as support for other people's ideas. The problem is that the other people don't always have good ideas.

Without help, IT groups often do the wrong thing. They build systems that do not end up delivering enough value to justify their cost. It is not that IT groups cannot create prioritized lists of projects that need to be done; it is that their criteria for prioritizing projects may not be the ones that will yield valuable systems. To be fair, most IT groups now include business analysts who figure out how to get projects to align with business goals. But the best analyst in the world is only as good as the support he gets from those in the organization who know what the business goals are and how each business unit can forward them.

What's the way out? Information management, of course!

Lead, Don't Practice

To lead information management practitioners, you do not have to be a practitioner. In fact, I have seen professional experience hurt leaders as much as it has helped them.

First, some leaders who can do the work of their staff actually end up doing the work of their staff. They secretly (or not so secretly) miss and enjoy the programming, or design, or whatever else they used to do. They immerse themselves in detail and forget about the big picture they are supposed to be pushing. They forget, or never realize, that their concern is not how the work gets done, but what work gets done. Like the clan leader whose authority comes from being the strongest warrior, these supervisors often define authority as the ability to do the work better than anyone else. This approach undermines the confidence of your team and distracts you from your real job. If you are unsuccessful in this approach, you will likely lose authority and look like a fool to your staff. If you succeed, all work practice will revolve around you. The confidence of your team will remain low, and they will have no ability to scale beyond what you can do.

Second, some leaders who know too much about the details of the work cannot get their staff to look past the details. Conversation happens at much too tactical a level to ever address the bigger concerns of the group. If you are ignorant of the details (or at least pretend to be), you stand no chance of being drawn into and getting lost in the technical details of the projects. You can use this position of ignorance to demand that the terms of any discussion be the trans-discipline, strategic terms. When programmers talk code, or designers talk image, you can drag them back to the common territory of goals, audience, and information. The collection and dissemination of information is its own discipline with its own vocabulary and rules. If you do not stand up for that discipline, who will?

 Should we bring in a set of vendors to demo?

 Sure, but then I assume you have a full requirements set for what this system is supposed to do. I assume that the requirements are derived from the information, audiences, authors, sources, channels, processes, and publications the system will require. Can I see the script that all venders will follow to show that they have understood and can satisfy our specifications?

Finally, some leaders unwittingly favor the people in their teams with similar backgrounds. A leader who spent years as a network administrator will naturally have more to say to the administration staff than to, say, the editorial staff. The dialogue of the group as a whole tends to skew toward the leader's discipline, and power tends to congregate there.

Of course professional experience is good. It's just not all it is cracked up to be. If you have solid professional experience, it can be a valuable backdrop to your real job. However, you will have to consciously transcend it if you want to get all the disciplines to come together. There's nothing like the joy and glory of "calling BS" on a professional or suggesting the winning system design. But these joys are secondary to your real job: making an impact on the organization's goals.

Boot Up a Strategic Project Evaluation Process

How should you view project proposals that are brought to you? Without, or before a strategy, what other tools do you have to help you decide what sort of resources you should commit? It may be a while before a well-founded set of criteria (based on a well-founded strategy) will begin to sink into the minds of the people who suggest projects. People will not immediately begin to apply the standards themselves and will not automatically stop present strategic justifications. While you boot-up strategy, you will have to continue to respond to ongoing projects and new proposals.

To head off unproductive projects and prepare your staff and peers for the strategy that is to come, you can establish project justification criteria. As you might suspect, the criteria should be the same as those the strategy will be based on: goals, audiences, and information. If you begin requiring this sort of justification today, it will not only help you identify unjustified projects, it will also train project initiators to begin thinking strategically and provide great input into your developing strategy.

If you do no more than ask project leaders to tell you what goals, audiences, and information they intend to serve, you will be off to a good start. If you also require them to justify that the ones they have chosen, you will have all you need to begin to judge the worthiness of proposed and ongoing projects. Finally, if you require project leaders to relate the goals, audiences, and information types they have chosen to those already in play in other systems or projects, they will be forced to judge for themselves how valuable their projects are in the context of other players.

It's up to you how far and how fast to take this idea. You can derive a lot of input to your strategy and get your staff completely up-to-speed on strategy by requiring a thorough justification from each team. On the other hand, this exercise might generate confusion and anxiety. I would be most tempted to do such a thorough justification regime across all projects if I had just taken charge. In this situation, you need input, and no one would be surprised if you asked for a comprehensive rejustification of projects.

Even if you decide to employ them casually, these justifications can be used to your advantage as you discuss projects. You can stir the pot and begin introducing a new mode of thinking.

Review Your Project Portfolio

To deserve support, a project has to be at least as important as the other projects you are doing to advance your goals. As I have mentioned, importance is measured in terms of the audiences, goals, and information a project concerns. If you have many projects in process, and especially if many of those projects don't seem as important as the ones you want to do, it may be worthwhile to review the full portfolio to determine the value of every ongoing project. At the end of the review, you can allocate funds to projects based on overall strategic value.

This process, as I'm sure you already know, can seem threatening to your staff. People are committed to their projects, and the process of a general review carries with it the possibility of project terminations. If you have a clear, convincing strategy and a way to impartially judge projects against that strategy, no matter how nervous your staffers might become, they can't argue that they deserve to be funded over projects that are more valuable to the organization. If you have already been asking them to justify their own projects, then they will also have had ample opportunity to build their cases when the full review finally begins.

Reign In Scope

Obviously, you will not want to totally shut down current projects or totally discourage new projects. Instead, you should try to optimize projects and proposals to push them, at first gently, in the right direction.

There are a few simple questions you can ask of a project to help perform this "optimization":

- **Information is expensive**. Can you handle less information and still reach the same result for the organization?

- **How much leverage** is there between the audiences that you are serving? Is there much overlap in the information they require? Do they all want to get their information the same way? Can you serve fewer types or more closely related types of people and get the same result?

- **Can your project be modified to serve a narrower goal?** Should you aim a bit lower to diminish risk and live within more modest project budget and scope?

I like these questions because they are simple but incisive. Many people who come with project proposals mistakenly think that bigger is better. To them, the size (pages, database records, files, or whatever) really matters. Thus, they naturally try to include as much information in the system as possible. Similarly, they mistakenly believe that their system will be for everyone and that they are serving the widest goals.

By questioning these assumptions, you drive the projects that you review toward increased efficiency. In many cases, as you discard the information that cannot be linked to goals, the system dips below a size that justifies building a system at all. The truly strategic information in the proposal could just be handled manually. You should always be ready to suggest that option gently. Tighter clustering of audiences can make a system much simpler and cheaper to build. Similarly, serving more specific goals can lead to smaller systems with a value that is much easier to establish.

Establish Project Checkpoints

The centerpiece and hallmark of your information-management leadership within your group could be project checkpoint meetings. It is a great way to involve yourself at just the right level and in just the right way with the projects. Whether a project proposal originates from your team or from you, at some point, the planning of the project will be in the hands of the project team. Checkpoints provide a way to have a productive part in projects while giving teams a series of compelling events with which to mark the progress.

Project Start

There is usually no problem instilling a project team with a sense of ownership of the technical and architectural aspects of a project. A project kickoff checkpoint is a great way to instill them as well with ownership of the strategic and informational aspects of the project. During this brief meeting, you can ask the team to present its argument for why this project is important based on the established strategy. You can also ask them to provide an overview of the information content of the project and how they expect to collect and tag it. If you really want to put teeth into your oversight of projects, you can ask the team to commit to specific measurable targets for the goals they are addressing.

Project Midterm

Once a project is under way, teams tend to stop looking at the big picture as they get mired in the details and trade-offs of implementation. The sum total of the little decisions they make can often change the basic focus of the system. During this part of a project, you can set up a checkpoint where you ask key questions to determine if the project is going to advance goals. This checkpoint is intended to be the event that compels the team to reground the value of their system. Some of the questions that you might ask include:

- How has your definition of the audience changed since you started this project? If it has changed, should it trigger a change in your strategy? Should it change the importance of the project?

- Are you confident that you will hit the targets that you committed to for the goals the project addresses? Can we raise the targets?

- What leverage do you see for the other projects that serve the same audience, information, or distribution channel? What are the implications for the group that is supplying information?

- Exactly how much information will the system launch with and how much will it process over time? Are you sure how much effort it will take to launch and maintain the information? Who will do this work?

- What productivity tools are you developing for this project? Are they justified by time-savings? Can they be leveraged to other projects? (See the "Destroy the Myth of Future Returns and General Solutions" section in Chapter 14, Set the Tone of the Department.)

- What help do you need making sure that the information contributors hold up their side of the bargain? If you have done your work, you will be just the one to assist if there are problems (see "Proactively Approach Groups" in Chapter 11, Engage Intelligently).

It's important that these meetings not be pro forma. They will work to the extent that you are personally committed to comparing your understanding of the strategy to the understanding gained by your team when they try to implement it. While you are serving as judge to the team, they will do so as well for you and your strategy. If you work hard during these encounters, they can become your main tool for testing and refining your strategy. But don't expect your team to understand that. To them, these meetings will at best be like midterm exams and at worst like inquisitions.

Project End

I've attended a lot of project postmortem sessions. They are fine but often lead to nothing. The problem is that there is no real way to generalize the lessons learned. The individual team members get a lot out of deconstructing the project, but the department as a whole does not fare as well. You can deal with the wider implications of a project by having the team make specific reference to your strategy. You can compare the gains predicted by the project against the gains you will actually realize. You can also have the team suggest how the project could have been construed to better meet its goals.

But most importantly, because the project is done (for better or for worse), you can ask for explicit strategy and tactic criticisms, extensions, and other suggestions based on the project. At this stage of a project, people are usually in the right frame of mind to perceive broader implications.

Project checkpoints establish you as the one to please. If pleasing you means advancing your strategy, then checkpoints are a great way to assure that the strategy is advanced. In addition, you can use checkpoints as a tool to review and evolve your strategy. Checkpoints give you a simple, easy-to-use method that puts you in the center of every project without challenging its ownership or management. It does not require much time, and it returns big rewards. Checkpoints keep your projects on track with your strategy and keep your strategy on track with reality.

Originate Projects

Once you have a strategy in place, judging projects becomes much simpler. Good projects cover much of the strategy that is currently not covered, and bad ones do not. Of course, you will have to get a bit more specific in your formulation, but the idea remains uncomplicated. More importantly than judging projects, a strategy allows you to suggest and commission projects. You can drive all projects by setting the standard for what a good project is and does.

Nonstrategic Projects

A nonstrategic project has no direct correlation with the goals of your organization. That does not necessarily mean that the project is not worth doing, however; it does mean that if you choose to do the project, you will have fewer resources left to do the projects that are directly correlated with goals. Here some reasons you might choose to do a nonstrategic project:

- **It is small**. I'd recommend being wary of this justification. If (or when) the project expands to two or three times its estimated schedule or budget, will you still consider it small enough to fly under the strategic radar?

- **It is diplomatic**. The project buys good relations with a key group or individual. In these cases, you are willing to spend some resources now against support or resources you might ask the same people for later. You might want to check twice that such a project does not cost you more than it returns. You might also consider forming an agreement that makes the *quid pro quo* explicit.

- **It proves something**. Small projects that demonstrate a methodology (ad-hoc workflow, for example), delivery channel (wikis, for example), technology, or other contentious issues can be worth doing prior to committing to them in a "real" project. In these cases, I suggest not using real information delivered to real people (unless, of course, that is what you are testing). It is easy to end up with a system that does not prove what it set out to do because it gets bogged down by the demands of delivering real content.

- **It will provide greater productivity**. These projects, which produce tools rather than systems, should be evaluated strictly on the basis of your return on investment (ROI). I am astonished how many great tool ideas don't end up returning on their investments. Between the inevitable scope creep and the wage difference between the creators and the users of the tool, it is easy to lose money and productivity on a productivity tool (see "Destroy the Myth of Future Returns and General Solutions" in Chapter 14, Set the Tone of the Department, for more on this perspective).

- **It is fun and interesting**. Before you impose a strict project justification process on your teams, consider how much "cool stuff" they get to do now. If you drive out all the inefficient projects, will you drive out all the interesting work with it? Will your most creative folks leave along with the fun? Why not explicitly recognize the value of these sorts of project to your staff and even use them as a reward for having completed projects with indisputable business value?

There should always be some room in your project schedule for experimentation, prototyping, special projects, skunk works, and plain fun. As long as the bulk of your projects make solid headway against goals, you can afford to splurge a little on other stuff. And, of course, in the long run, it is just these marginal sorts of projects that will lead to the most creative, innovative solutions to the big problems.

Be the Information Guys

When someone needs expertise or help "doing" information,
your group should be the natural place to go. You know what it
means to do information and can help them do it right.

For most IT groups, technology is what they know, it is what they like, and it is what they are prepared to deliver. That's fine, really. We need good technology guys (and gals, of course) because, as they say, "whatever else you are doing, you are also doing computers!" Being the technology guys is fine, as far as it goes. Unfortunately, it does not go far enough. Information technology groups now really need to be the information guys as well as the technology guys.

Claim the mandate and be the source of
information wisdom and practice.

What does it mean to be the information guys? More than anything else, it means claiming and then owning the "information territory." The information territory includes knowing what information means strategically to the organization, how individual groups should produce, amass, and distribute information in accordance with that strategy, and having practical advice and effective tools for helping people identify and distribute good information.

When someone needs expertise or help "doing" information, your group is the natural place to go. You know what it means to "do" information and can help other groups do it right. You are a key part of information management projects, and you have earned enough respect that people with projects want you on board.

As the chief information guy, you are the first to recognize and promote the idea that information itself is a subject of concern. Information has structure in the form of a narrative, complex argument with claims and warrants. It has a layout, design, a tone, and a voice. It has an author whose motives consumers seek to uncover and myriad other aspects to be accounted for and understood. Information has a lot going on. We have been used to leaving all this complexity to the writers and editors, but no more. If you are to take charge of information, then the structure of information will also have to be your concern.

The information guys are service people. My favorite example of the kind of service that information people could provide is Radar O'Reilly from the book, movie, and TV show *MASH*. Radar's hallmark is his ability to anticipate the needs of his audience (his commanding officer) and have the information ready before the CO even knows he needs it.

Radar is the ideal information guy. He knows his audience so well that he can anticipate needs that have yet to even be articulated. He is the complete master of his information base. The exact right item of information is forever at his fingertips. He delivers information with accuracy and precision that are unrivaled by any conceivable computer system. Of course, he does so because he is fictional. Even the best executive secretary could never match his performance. But that's OK. Radar is an ideal to strive for, not an example to follow. As you strive to master information management, Radar stands out there on the horizon like a beacon. What can you do to know your audiences so well that you can anticipate information needs before they are even articulated? How can your systems locate and deliver information to the exact point of use?

A more plausible example of a true information guy is the reference librarian. If you have never walked into a library and asked an obscure or off-the-wall question, give it a try. What you will find is someone who may know nothing about your subject but is nonetheless able to find an enormous amount of relevant and authoritative information about it. How can you deliver the same level of service to the people who are most important to your organization's goals?

The information guys see every problem as an information problem. As my friend and mentor Mike Eisenberg, former Dean of the University of Washington iSchool, says, they "see the world through information-colored glasses." Whatever else you are doing, you are also creating and delivering information.

The information guys know how to use information. If they didn't, then why would anyone else trust them? Everyone says information is power, but the information guys demonstrate it. They find good answers within the organization and on the Web. Not only do they tell other people how to turn their information into a powerful force for business benefit, they do it themselves. Their own internal information always seems to be at the right place at the right time to forward their own goals. In presentations, facilitation, and reports, their information is high quality, timely, and pertinent. This does not mean that the information guys have to have a lot of expensive systems that store and deliver all information. In fact, they have the minimum amount of fancy technology needed to ensure that their most important information is collected and delivered for maximum benefit. The information guys wield information and show the rest of the organization the power that derives from its directed use.

In a room with the marketing guy, the finance guy, the operations guy, and all the other guys, the information guy has a place. At the very least, she can add an information perspective to the other perspectives in the room. At the best, she can lead every group of which she is a part. On the strength of her ideas and ability to be at the center of every issue and working all its angles, she can bring any group into alignment on a solution. Add a well-coordinated team of information guys behind her, and the information guy can be the most effective guy in the room.

You can make your group be the information guys if you want to. You can build respect and expertise. It's tough, but it is no harder than what any other group does to remake itself as its environment changes. But ask yourself, "Does an information attitude fit me and my team?" It's okay if it is a foreign attitude; we are capable of learning new attitudes. But it's not okay if it is an attitude you don't understand or can't see yourself adopting. If you (and your key team members) don't really want to be the information guys, there is no point in going down this path. Turn over your "I" to a group that wants it.

On the other hand, if you are willing and able to take up the mantle of information and firmly weld an "I" to your group's "T," you can expand your relevance, increase the effectiveness of your projects, and enhance your influence within your organization. History is on the side of information. Eventually we will all learn to treat it as the resource it could be. You can be forgotten by that history, or you can help to make it.

About the Author

Bob Boiko is founder and president of Metatorial Services Inc., and is a faculty member of the University of Washington Information School. He lives with his wife and two sons in Seattle, Washington, USA.

Recognized worldwide as a leader in the field of content management, he has almost 20 years of experience designing and building Web, hypertext, and multimedia systems and tools for some of the world's top technology corporations (including Microsoft, Motorola, and Boeing). Bob has sat on many advisory boards and is the recipient of many awards including the 2005 EContent 100 Award for leadership in the content management industry. He is author of two editions of *Content Management Bible* as well as this book. Bob is internationally known for his lectures and workshops. In 2004, Bob sparked the creation of CM Professionals, the first and only content management organization for practitioners

Metatorial Services is a micro consultancy, specializing in content and information management strategy and design. With a range of commercial, governmental, and nonprofit clients of every size, Metatorial Services has worked on just about every aspect of information management.

The University of Washington's Information School is a group dedicated to helping shape the emerging electronic information discipline. At the iSchool, Bob has trained hundreds of information professionals and designed and led programs in information leadership, systems design, and content management. Bob's academic interests include metadata, business analysis, information initiative planning, information architecture, information system design, and public access to information.

Bob is an extremely skilled analyst, facilitator, teacher, designer, and architect and has extensive expertise in content and knowledge management, authoring, multimedia design, Web publishing, and tool construction. He has undergraduate degrees in physics and oceanography and a graduate degree in human communication.

Before Metatorial Services, Bob co-founded Chase Bobko Inc. and built it into a leading content management service provider. Within Chase Bobko, Bob served as President, Head of Development, Head of Sales and Marketing, and Head of Operations. Bob and his partners grew Chase Bobko from a staff of six to a staff of more than 100.

Bob can be reached by e-mail at bob@metatorial.com.

Index

More Great Books from Information Today, Inc.

Making Search Work
Implementing Web, Intranet and Enterprise Search

By Martin White

This important book is designed to help organizations understand, evaluate, and implement desktop, Web site, intranet, and enterprise search applications. Martin White explains search technology in clear, nontechnical language and describes the benefits and issues for a range of solutions—from high-end to affordable plug-and-play software products. In addition to providing critical guidance, the book features a glossary, suggestions for further reading, and an annotated listing of firms providing Web, intranet, and enterprise search solutions.

192 pp/hardbound/ISBN 978-1-57387-305-5 $69.50

Information Management for the Intelligent Organization, 3rd Edition

By Chun Wei Choo

The intelligent organization is one that is skilled at marshaling its information resources, transforming information into knowledge, and using it to sustain and enhance its performance in a restless environment. Chun Wei Choo explains how organizations can manage information processes more effectively in order to achieve these goals.

272 pp/hardbound/ISBN 978-1-57387-125-9 $39.50

Smart Services
Competitive Information Strategies, Solutions, and Success Stories for Service Businesses

By Deborah C. Sawyer

This is the first book to focus specifically on the competitive information needs of service-oriented firms. Author, entrepreneur, and business consultant Deborah C. Sawyer illuminates the many forms of competition in service businesses, identifies the most effective information resources for competitive intelligence (CI), and provides a practical framework for identifying and studying competitors in order to gain a competitive advantage. *Smart Services* is a road map for every service company owner, manager, or executive who expects to compete effectively in the Information Age.

CyberAge Books/256 pp/softbound/ISBN 978-0-910965-56-9 $29.95

Net Crimes & Misdemeanors, 2nd Edition
Outmaneuvering Web Spammers, Stalkers, and Con Artists

By J. A. Hitchcock
Foreword by Vint Cerf

In this revised and expanded edition of her popular book, cybercrime expert J. A. Hitchcock offers practical and easy-to-follow methods for dealing with spam, viruses, hack attacks, identity theft, and other online dangers. The book covers a broad range of abusive practices and features dozens of firsthand anecdotes and success stories. A one-time victim of cyberstalking who fought back and won, Hitchcock went on to become a leading victim's advocate. Her readable and reassuring book is loaded with tips, strategies, and techniques as well as pointers to the laws, organizations, and Web resources that can aid victims and help them fight back. Supported by a Web page.

CyberAge Books/496 pp/softbound/ISBN 0-910965-72-2 $24.95

Understanding and Communicating Social Informatics

A Framework for Studying and Teaching the Human Contexts of Information and Communication Technologies

By Rob Kling, Howard Rosenbaum, and Steve Sawyer

Here is a sustained investigation into the human contexts of information and communication technologies (ICTs), covering both research and theory. The authors demonstrate that the design, adoption, and use of ICTs are deeply connected to people's actions as well as to the environments in which ICTs are used. They offer a pragmatic overview of social informatics, articulating its fundamental ideas for specific audiences and presenting important research findings.

240 pp/hardbound/ISBN 978-1-57387-228-7 $39.50

Knowledge Management Lessons Learned

What Works and What Doesn't

Edited by Michael E. D. Koenig and T. Kanti Srikantaiah

A follow-up to Srikantaiah and Koenig's ground-breaking *Knowledge Management for the Information Professional* (2000), this new book surveys recent applications and innovation in KM. More than 30 experts describe KM in practice, revealing what has been learned, what works, and what doesn't. Includes projects undertaken by organizations at the forefront of KM, and coverage of KM strategy and implementation, cost analysis, education and training, content management, communities of practice, competitive intelligence, and much more.

624 pp/hardbound/ISBN 978-1-57387-181-5 $44.50

Theories of Information Behavior

Edited by Karen E. Fisher, Sanda Erdelez, and Lynne (E. F.) McKechnie

Here are authoritative overviews of more than 70 conceptual frameworks for understanding how people seek, manage, share, and use information in different contexts. Covering established and proposed theories, the book includes contributions from 85 scholars from 10 countries. Theory descriptions cover origins, propositions, methodological implications, usage, and links to related theories.

456 pp/hardbound/ISBN 978-1-57387-230-0 $49.50

The Visible Employee
Using Workplace Monitoring and Surveillance to Protect Information Assets—Without Compromising Employee Privacy or Trust

By Jeffrey M. Stanton and Kathryn R. Stam

Organizations are increasingly monitoring employee usage of network resources including the Web—but how well are they doing? Based on an extensive four-year research project, *The Visible Employee* reports on a range of security solutions and the attitudes of employees toward workplace surveillance. A must-read for managers, IT staff, and employees with privacy concerns.

CyberAge Books/376 pp/softbound/ISBN 978-0-910965-74-3 $24.95